THE THRICE SHY

Cultural accommodation
to blindness and other disasters
in a Mexican community

THE THRICE SHY

*Cultural accommodation
to blindness and other disasters
in a Mexican community*

JOHN L. GWALTNEY

1970

Columbia University Press
NEW YORK AND LONDON

John L. Gwaltney is Associate Professor of Anthropology at the State University of New York, College at Cortland.

To insure anonymity, care has been taken to avoid any correlation between the actual names of informants and the initials used in this work. J.L.G.

LIBRARY OF CONGRESS CATALOG CARD NUMBER: *71-118635*
INTERNATIONAL STANDARD BOOK NUMBER: *0-231-03237-4*

Printed in the United States of America

PREFACE AND ACKNOWLEDGMENTS

This work is the product of data amassed during the field phase of the National Institutes of Mental Health Project, "Role of expectation of blindness in a Oaxaca village."

Data were gathered from May of 1963 through March of 1964 in the Chinantec-speaking village of San Pedro Yolox in southeastern Mexico. The research was supported by National Institutes of Mental Health Grant Number 5–FL–MH–16,788.

As co-principal investigator of this project, which was under the general direction of Dr. Margaret Mead, Curator of Ethnology of the American Museum of Natural History and Adjunct Professor of Anthropology at Columbia University, the author conducted ethnographic research with special reference to the blinding, fly-borne disease known variously as onchocerciasis, Robles' disease, or river blindness, in a general stressful environment. The latter degenerative course of this filarial infestation, known locally as *mal de la ceguera,* or the blinding sickness, is but one of a variety of stressful agencies which constitute a customary stressful climate.

The prevailing belief that filarially induced blindness is the consequence of omnipotent, arbitrary, divine intervention tends toward the emergence of an essentially accommodative cultural response. The transgenerational link between the elderly onchocercous blind and child guides, the role of mendicancy in the maintenance of a sense of participation on the part of the blind, the ascription of ritual efficacy and public merit to deferential behavior toward blind persons, the obverse ascription of strong supernatural and social opprobrium to undeferential behavior toward them, and the absence of curative traits from indigenous medical technology and sorcery are indicative of an essentially accommodative adjustment to blindness.

Control and eradication, the response of greater Mexican medical technology to onchocerciasis, exceeds the prevailing indigenous concept of the possible. The standard course of treatment superimposed by the dominant state currently necessitates the addition of negative elements, therapeutic shock and minor surgery, to an already extensive accretion of environmental trauma.

The indigenous subculture's accommodative response emerges from the transgenerational conditioning of a formidable roster of negative expectations in a traditional context of pervasive poverty. This fundamental disparity between the respective cultural definitions of the realm of possibility and the negative aspects associated with the standard course of treatment are instrumental factors in the massive resistance encountered by the Mexican government's National Campaign against Onchocerciasis.

I am keenly and gratefully aware of the uncommon exertions of many persons in my behalf. From pre-field orientation through preparation of the doctoral thesis from which this book is derived, Dr. Margaret Mead has generously proffered both advice and assistance.

For his unfailing advice and encouragement from the very inception of my graduate academic career I am profoundly indebted to Mr. Philip G. Trupin of the New Jersey Commission for the Blind.

A number of scholars, Dr. Rhoda Métraux of the American Museum of Natural History, Dr. Eric Wolf of the Department of Anthropology of the University of Michigan, Dr. John Crawford, Dr. Benjamin Elson, Mr. Frank Robbins, and Mr. W. C. Townsend of the Summer Institute of Linguistics, Mitla, Oaxaca, contributed generously to the pre-field consultations regarding choice of site and the general feasibility of the project.

Dr. Howard F. Cline, Director of the Hispanic Foundation of the Library of Congress contributed to the pre-field consultations and generously offered advice and assistance relating to the rather specialized literature pertaining to the Chinantec. Mr. Paul R. Palmer, Librarian of the Burgess-Carpenter Library at Columbia University, was instrumental in the acquisition and prolonged use of library materials, thereby facilitating the vital work of braille transcription.

I am under the most profound obligation to Dr. Julio de la Fuente of the Instituto Nacional Indigenista whose advice and assistance in both the pre-field and initial phases of field orientation were invaluable and never-failing.

I am grateful to Professor Conrad M. Arensberg of the Department of Anthropology of Columbia University and to Visiting Professor Octavio Ianni of the Institute of Latin American Studies of that university for reading this manuscript and for their advice and assistance in its final preparation.

Special thanks are due the Nahmad family, especially Sr. Salomón Nahmad, whose advice and assistance as guide were invaluable in my orientation to Oaxaca and the district of Ixtlán. In this connection, special thanks are also due to Dr. Santiago Barahona Streber of Mitla and to Sr. Dario Toro Quero, Curator of the Museo Frisell de Arte Zapoteco de Mitla.

Prior to and during the entire field phase of the project the ordering, interpretation, and resolution of the administrative aspect of the project were in the sensitive and capable hands of Dr. Julia G. Crane of the University of North Carolina.

I am especially indebted to Dr. John C. Saunders for medical advice and supplies which proved to be indispensable in the field.

For invaluable assistance in the acquisition and expedition of field equipment I am greatly indebted to Dr. Victor Novick, Mr. Kenneth Milligan, and to Mr. Robert Gwaltney.

I am deeply appreciative of the diverse vital contributions of readers, researchers, and braillists. In this regard I feel bound to mention the especially vital contributions of Mrs. Diana Beachum, Dr. Nancy Bowers, Mr. Robert Buedingen, Miss Henrietta Bystock, Miss Janet Carter, Mrs. Lucy Fletcher, Dr. Dexter Jeannotte, Mrs. Augusta Souza Kappner, Mr. Thomas M. H. Kappner, Dr. Mary MacDonald, Mr. Cecilio Martinez, Mrs. Bridget Merle, Mr. Michel Merle, Mrs. Gwendolyn Novick, Dr. Theodore Schwartz, Mrs. Cherry Vayda, and Mr. James Yohannan.

Training in the vital field skill of riding and the burden of library research are only two of the indispensable contributions of my wife, Judith, to this project.

Photographs taken in the field inspired the sensitive illustrations which were created for this book by Mr. James Bartow. Special thanks also are due to Professor John Willmer for his cartographic advice and assistance.

Father Gonzalo Guerrero Quintero, the village priest, and Srta. Maria Pilar Santiago Reyes, who directed the village Health Center, gave generously of their time and advice and accorded access to ecclesiastical archives and medical records.

Needless to say, this book could not have been written without the general cooperation, confidence and gracious acceptance of the villagers among whom I was privileged to live and work. A special debt of gratitude is due Don Federico López Velasco and Don Daniel Hernandez Bautista, presidents during my stay in the village, and Don Apolinar Bautista Martinez and Don Jorge Martín de Vidal, municipal secretaries. Doña Rebeca Mendoza de Vidal, Doña Margarita Bautista Hernandez, Doña Margarita Pérez, Srta. Margarita Bautista Martinez, Don Vicente López Pérez, Don Paulino Bautista, Don Pedro Hernandez Mendoza, and Don Pedro López Mendoza are but a few of the many who contributed the data which are the basis of this book. The debt of gratitude owed Don Felícitos López Pérez, the knowledgeable and tactful gentleman who served me so well as friend, guide and assistant, is beyond estimation.

CONTENTS

ix

LIST OF MAPS

LIST OF TABLES

THE THRICE SHY

Cultural accommodation
to blindness and other disasters
in a Mexican community

*In moving to understand the systematic character of the life
of the community the student cannot begin everywhere; he
must begin at some point. What shall that point be? Commonly the beginning is made with the things immediately
visible.*   [REDFIELD 1960:19]

Being unable to begin my attempt to understand San
Pedro Yolox and its highland Chinantec population upon
the basis of "the things immediately visible," I was
obliged to rely upon the audible evidence for my point of
departure—more especially the auditory rhythms of the
pueblo. The lulls in the summer-long roaring of the swol-
len streams which promise a break in the rains; the slow,
sonorous emergence and recession of the death knell amid
conventional occasions for bell ringing; the ragged crackle
of the heavy Belgian rifles in the hands of the soldiers
during the occasional target sessions which emphasize the
inadvisability of any breach of the Pax Mexicana; the
escalation in the more or less constant canine din which
heralds the arrival of a stranger; the alternation of com-

fortable domestic Chinantec speech (*idioma*) and official, imported *Castillano*;* the fluctuation in the general noise level which indicates the congregation and dispersal of the villagers at such points of village interaction as the laundering place, the stores, the atrium of the church, and the schoolyard—all these sound patterns reflect Chinantec culture and environment.

Many of the sounds of life proceeding in the context of the pueblo were unintelligible to me and had to be explained by villagers who took them for granted. The general willingness to attempt such explanations (no villager ever ignored a request for amplification), coupled with the difficulty most of the same people experienced in communicating about the less specific, nonmaterial aspects of their culture, assisted in my interpretation of it.

Villagers were intent upon acquiring insight into my culture. Their numerous inquiries centered on specific, physical traits of that culture: my iron canes, my "finger" watch, my "finger" reading, my ubiquitous tape recorder, my typewriter and my "finger writing machine." Indeed, almost everything I owned was the subject of keen interest. Less than an hour after my arrival in the village I had rhetorical evidence that even in this remote corner of the Sierra Juárez news of a dominant flaw in my own society had preceded me.

Let me hasten to assure you of one thing. You are our brother. The radio brings us the barbarous news from Alabama and other parts of the United States where such atrocious crimes are committed against the people of your color. We are a poor people and many of us do not have much education, but

* In common Mexican usage the Spanish language is often referred to as Castilian.

we have that natural wisdom which God gives even the humblest of His children. So there is no one among us who would demean himself by abusing another human being simply because his skin is darker. Set your mind at ease for you are in your pueblo among your people. [MUNICIPAL SECRETARY'S WELCOMING ADDRESS, FIELD NOTES]

A number of villagers were interested in my personal and communal status in my own society. Our respective curiosity set in motion a voluminous flow of inquiry and clarifying discourse. This exchange also had its pulse, for gradually those villagers properly reckoned as knowledgeable repositories of the culture emerged.

Many of the resource informants singled out for intense consultation were onchocercous blind persons. These knowledgeable senior men, assured of the respectful attention of an attentive junior, cigarettes and an ever-filled cup, were admirable subjects for open-ended interviews.

The *Ayuntamiento,* or village government, graciously accorded me access to the municipal archives. A number of young men with optimum educations by local standards extracted data from these files. In addition to the valuable supplement to oral inquiry subsequently derived from these documents, the leisurely, egalitarian atmosphere of the work session afforded an opportunity for intense interviews of resource informants drawn from the generation of young married males. Resident non-Chinantec persons (the priest and his family and the nurse at the Health Center) were also generous in donating their valuable time and access to records.

Village children were the first Yoleños I encountered on the steep, stepped trail to the pueblo. They came to offer to "walk," that is, to act as guides. They came accompanying and guiding senior resource informants who are their friends or their biological or ritual kin. They played and explained their games, told their dreams, exchanged such local delicacies as grasshoppers in scalded milk for conventional hard candy, and acted as informants in a very free context.

My sense of the quality and tenor of Chinantec life is derived from what I heard and my understanding of what I heard. And my understanding of what I heard was amplified and refined by many bilingual villagers of both sexes and all ages who rendered me the same courteous service of translation which they extend to their monolingual fellow villagers.

Upon my arrival in the village, I made a gift of mescal to the Honorable Ayuntamiento. The members of that body responded with a gift of beer and a number of welcoming addresses. These hours of well-spiked conviviality served to clarify at the outset my reasons for coming to the pueblo. My hosts, all men of substance, defined anthropology and the work of a student of that profession in a number of unusual but serviceable ways. For it seems that some notion of that discipline had preceded me via the same medium which had borne the bad news from Alabama. The several definitions, for all their diversity, had three things in common: anthropology had something to do with studying people, an anthropologist need not be a handy fellow with a shovel, and students of that discipline had no mandate or desire to dose, tax, convert, or coerce anybody.

As my stay in the village lengthened into months and my daily walks multiplied by tens, scores, and hundreds, the leathery creaking of the wooden cane mill, the whistled commands to beasts of burden, the monotonous powdery muffled thumping of the heavy wooden hammer falling on the dugout orange log half full of coffee beans, and the omnipresent sound of coughing assumed the quality of the customary.

For all its remoteness and inaccessibility, the village of San Pedro Yolox is possessed of a roster of recommendations as a site for ethnographic purposes which in some degree compensates for the rigorous quality of physical existence there. In the first place the village is small enough for one observer to get to know it. As an administrative unit, the Mexican *municipio* is roughly analogous to the North American county. The village bears roughly the same relationship to the rest of the municipio that the county seat bears to the environing territory of a county. The eighth Mexican decennial census reckons the population of the entire subdivision at 1,987. The locus of this study was the *cabecera,* or county seat of the entire subdivision. The village *Lista de los habitantes,* a village maintained registry of "all who walk with us," numbers the "sons of the pueblo" and their dependents wherever they may reside within the political subdivision at 973.

Pounding coffee beans in a hollow log.

The central location of the village in the Oaxaca onchocerciasis zone, a very high onchocerciasis infection rate,
and the largest onchocercous blind population of the entire
Oaxaca endemic focus made San Pedro Yolox an admirable site. There is a rough linear centrality in the village
settlement pattern. Though frequently verging on the ver-
tical and qualified by isolating hollows, ravines, and cas-
cades, this linear centrality was more a feature of the
Yoleño settlement pattern than it was of other potential
sites investigated. This relative proximity of houses and
house clusters is an invaluable asset to any observer, but
more especially to anyone obliged to hear his way.

In *their* pueblo on their own ground, the Yolox Chinantec are a reserved but not a taciturn people. A conventional surface amiability characterizes daily interaction.
Public courtesy in speech is an expectation and children
learn it with their language. The maintenance of this
public posture is the mark of a properly reared child, a
lady, a gentleman, or an anthropologist worth bothering
with. There are a number of conventional ways of expressing common conversational themes. Jocular, imaginative, individualistic informality is a quality of conversation among friends. Concurrent with my increasing
understanding of and accommodation to the quality of
Yoleño culture there was a plainly perceptible increase
in those conversational styles beyond mere public courtesy. When engaging in conversation in a context of intimate amity, the grief, rage, elation, awe, or chagrin which
are so muted and indirect in conventional communication
find strong, individual expression which approaches the
poetic.

During such open interviews many informants often

made statements that were apt and indicative of general Yoleño Chinantec ethos. Some of these representative statements have been culled from my taped, brailled, and typewritten field notes and employed in this work to afford some Yoleños an opportunity to speak for their own culture.

When some main insights relative to the general life style of the village had been acquired, it was possible to frame and administer questionnaires pertaining to the specific areas of investigation. All these data—recorded biographies, loosely structured interviews, group discussions, festive and prosaic interaction, responses to questionnaires, precedence tales, rhetoric, music, children's games, civics lessons, and gossip preserved via the braillewriter, the typewriter, the tape recorder and a pair of attentive, accessible ears are the primary sources of this book.

Here our land is very ugly—nothing but mountains and trees. [M. L. FIELD NOTES]

The large and populous southeastern state of Oaxaca (95,364 square kilometers and 1,727,266 inhabitants according to the Mexican census of 1960) has been a primary area in both the pre-Columbian and post-contact history of Mexico. In terms of sheer diversity, Oaxaca is one of the richest Mexican ethnographic provinces. Of the 1,727,266 inhabitants, the 1960 census lists 297,319 persons as being indigenous monolinguals. Amuzgo, Cuicatec, Chatino, Chinantec, Huaxtec, Huave, Maya, Mazatec, Nahuatl, Mixe, Mixtec, Otomí, Popoluca, Zapotec and Zoque-speaking communities share this southern highlands area. Its populations reflect a similar genetic diversity. Contact occasioned a massive contribution of both Iberian Caucasoid and West African Negro genes into a basically Mongoloid Amerindian genetic reservoir (Wolf 1962:29–30).

Oaxaca as an ethnographic area is in turn subdivided

into a number of distinct regions distinguished for the provenience of a particular Amerindian group. Thus pueblos sharing the same name will be distinguished from one another by adding the appropriate Amerindian group. Thus it is proper to speak of the pueblo of Tiltepec, located in that part of the Sierra Juárez where Sierra Zapotecans are dominant, as Tiltepec Zapoteco. The pueblo of Tiltepec in the same general segment of the Sierra Madre Oriental where the Mixe are the dominant group is known as Tiltepec Mixe.

The state of Oaxaca is primarily the mid-section of the great Meso-American massif. The Sierra Madre Oriental extends from northwest to southeast through much of the state. The eastern extremity of Oaxaca is the relatively low arid continental waist of the Isthmus of Tehuantepec. The Sierra Madre Oriental runs the length of the northern, central, and south-central portions of the state, dividing it into a northern and a southern watershed.

The principal river systems having their origins on the southern slopes—Verde and Tehuantepec—traverse the narrow tropical southern coastal plain and discharge into the Pacific. The most important systems which rise on the northern flank—Papaloapan, Coatzacoalcos, and Uxpanapa—flow northward across the plain of Veracruz, debouching into the Gulf of Mexico and the Bay of Campeche.

San Pedro Yolox, the site of this field study, is located on that portion of this northern flank of the Oaxacan Sierra Madre Oriental called the Sierra Juárez. Yolox is a core area of an ill-defined ethnic subdivision known generally as the *Chinantla*. Depending upon their respective disciplinary points of departure, scholars have vari-

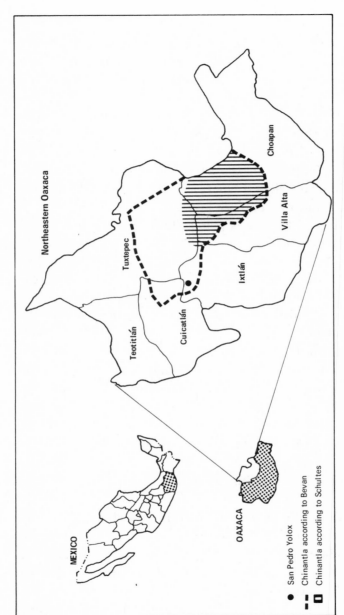

1. The Chinantla as delimited by Schultes and Bevan

(From Bernard Bevan. *The Chinantec.* Pan American Institute of Geography and History, 1938, p. 107, and Richard E. Schultes. "The Meaning and Usage of the Mexican Place-name 'Chinantla,'" Harvard University Botanical Museum Leaflet No. 9, 1941, p. 109.)

Legend:
- ● San Pedro Yolox
- ▬ ▬ Chinantla according to Bevan
- ▦ Chinantla according to Schultes

Map labels: MEXICO, OAXACA, Northeastern Oaxaca, Teotitlán, Tuxtepec, Cuicatlán, Ixtlán, Villa Alta, Choapan

ously defined the term *Chinantla*. Some (Gay 1933[I] :28; Espinosa 1961:78–93; Bevan 1938:10; Pérez García 1956[I] :96) subscribe to a delimitation which equates the geographical limits of the region with the demographic distribution of the Chinantec-speaking groups. By this widest definition the Chinantla would consist of portions of the following political subdivisions of northeastern Oaxaca: a small portion of the district of Villa Alta, most of the eastern third of the district of Cuicatlán, the northeastern limits of the district of Ixtlán, northern Choapam and a large portion of the district of Tuxtepec. Other scholars (Starr 1900:69; Schultes 1941:113–14) propose a somewhat more restricted definition. Dr. Schultes, for example, upon historical and botanical considerations, citing early contact documents, prefers to limit the region as follows. He proposes to restrict the term *Chinantla* to an area made up of the southern fringes of the districts of Tuxtepec, northern Choapam, and northeastern Villa Alta. By the former definition, the Chinantla would constitute a substantial part of northeastern Oaxaca. The latter delimitation would restrict the application of the term *Chinantla* largely to the rain forest area generally known as the southeastern, or lower, Chinantla. This latter restricted delimitation would exclude many northern and northwestern highland Chinantec-speaking areas from the Chinantla, including the site of this study. Map 1 illustrates the boundaries delimited by Bevan in 1938 and by Schultes in 1941.

However the Chinantla as a region is geographically proscribed, Americanists who have concerned themselves with the Chinantec as an ethnic group (Toor 1928; Lincoln 1939; Weitlaner 1939, 1940, 1951, 1964; Cruz 1946;

Ford 1948; I. Weitlaner 1952–53; Weitlaner and Castro 1954; Rubel 1955) appear to be in general accord with the classification set forth by Bevan. He divides the Chinantec-speaking population of northeastern Oaxaca into four subgroups. The Hu-me, or Valle Nacional subgroup, occupy the Valle Nacional between Yetla and Tuxtepec, including the small Chinantec-speaking group living along the upper San Cristóbal. A second lowland subgroup, called Wah-mi, occupy part of the district of Choapam. Among the principal Wah-mi villages are Lalana, Lovani, Petlapa, Tepinapa, and Teotalcingo. A third group, one of two highland segments, is the northern and western group whose principal centers are Usila, San Pedro Sochiapan and Ojitlán. This book deals with San Pedro Yolox, the core locality for the northwestern highland Chinantec-speaking group, the fourth group in Bevan's scheme and the seat of the ancient "kingdom" of Yoloxeniquila, or *los Yolos,* one of the two subdivisions of the highland Chinantla (Chinantla Pichinche) described in 1910 by Mariano Espinosa.*

The municipio of San Pedro Yolox is a small isolated political subdivision of the poor north Oaxacan district of Ixtlán. The municipio is a heavily forested, extremely mountainous cross-section of the steep northern escarpment of the Sierra Juárez. This precipitous 127.58 square kilometer tract extends downslope from southwest to northeast. Elevations in the municipio range from 710 meters above sea level at its lowest extremity in Rancho Esperanza to more than 2,000 meters above sea level in the ceremonial pueblo.

* See Appendix IV, Survey of the Literature Pertaining to the Chinantec.

The district of Ixtlán is a high, extremely mountainous 548.60 square kilometer area of northern Oaxaca peopled primarily by highland Chinantecans and Sierra Zapotecans. Some of its eminences rise almost 2 miles above sea level. Its northward inclining streams are tributary to the Papaloapan system (American Geographical Society 1959; Pérez García 1956[I] :185). The twenty-six municipios, or political subdivisions, of the district of Ixtlán are administered from the Sierra Zapotecan *cabecera*, or district seat, of Ixtlán de Juárez.

Scattered along the northern slopes of the Sierra Juárez, within the administrative jurisdiction of the district of Ixtlán, are a number of highland Chinantec communities. The municipio of San Pedro Yolox is one of these highland, northern escarpment Chinantec-speaking subdivisions of the district of Ixtlán. The municipio of San Pedro Yolox consists of a centrally situated pueblo or High Village and its environing hamlets and territory. The environing portions of this subdivision bear roughly the same relationship to the High Village as that seat does to the district center of Ixtlán de Juárez. The village of San Pedro Yolox is cabecera, that is, administrative center for the municipio of San Pedro Yolox, just as Ixtlán de Juárez is administrative center for the entire district of Ixtlán. Map 2 serves to demonstrate the location of Yolox within the district of Ixtlán and that district's location within the state of Oaxaca.

The highland Amerindian population of the municipio itself think of it as being divided into three natural provinces: *tierra fría, tierra templada,* and *tierra caliente.* The tierra fría, or cold region, is the high southeastern crest of the municipio. The dense evergreen forest area of

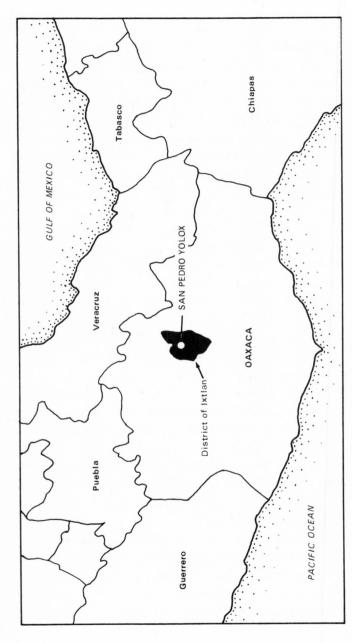

2. *Location of San Pedro Yolox in Southeastern Mexico*

this part of the municipio is the scene of some commercial lumber exploitation. There is some subsistence agriculture at this level also, but the steep inclination of the stony slope and the heavy forest cover place severe limits upon farming. There are three hamlets in this tierra fría: Temextitlán, San Martín Buena Vista, and San Francisco de la Reforma at altitudes above sea level of 2,100 meters at Temextitlán and 1,715 meters above sea level at San Francisco de la Reforma. San Martín Buena Vista is said by villagers to be higher than San Francisco and lower than Temextitlán. All of these *agencias,* or dependent hamlets, are under the juridical and administrative sovereignty of San Pedro Yolox. The major portion of the common lands lies in this coldest zone.

The High Village is the site of the municipal government, the one church of the municipio, and the only school in the municipio. The population of the pueblo fluctuates greatly. Most of the 973 Chinantec-speaking inhabitants are drawn in and dispersed in response to the *fiesta* round, the agricultural cycle, and the need to serve in the municipal government. There are a few families with land enough or commercial interests sufficient to sustain them in residence in the high pueblo throughout the year. It is rare that any more than one-fifth of the 130 dwellings of the central pueblo are occupied throughout the year.

Families who are especially anxious for their children to have a full year at school will often choose, at great cost to themselves, to remain in the central pueblo for as long as they can. Hunger generally obliges most of them to abandon the village for the downslope holdings in what the Chinantec of Yolox call *tierra caliente y húmeda* (hot, wet land), or *tierra buena* (good land).

The northern fifth of the municipio, especially the northeastern extremity is the hot, humid area from which the bulk of Yoleño subsistence is derived. Scattered downslope from the high pueblo to the northeast are seven small hamlets known collectively as *los ranchos* or *las rancherías*. It is here that the bulk of the agricultural activity is carried on. The forest is tropical and dense, separating these hamlets from each other. The people tend to think of them in this order: Rancho San Miguel, Rancho San Juan, Rancho Chirimoya, Rancho Esperanza, Rancho San Isidro, Rancho Bobo, and Rancho San Bernardo. The altitude of these hamlets varies from 1,120 meters above sea level in Rancho San Bernardo to 710 meters above sea level in Rancho Esperanza. It is in this extreme northeastern segment of the municipio that coffee, the only important cash crop, is cultivated.

It is also in the shaded springs and streams of this hot, humid, northeastern area that the blackflies which are the vector for onchocerciasis breed. Infection is unavoidable for the inhabitants of the municipio. The Mexican Campaign against Onchocerciasis in its pilot project to study and treat the disease, begun in September of 1960 and terminated in March of 1961, found that 49.4 percent of the inhabitants examined in Yolox were infected. The rate of infection in some of the low-lying ranchos was reported to be as high as 71.7 percent of the persons examined (Aranda Villamayor 1963:58). It has also been reported that there are nuclei of infection in the municipio which affect up to 90 percent of the total population (García Sánchez and Chávez Núñez 1962:950). The area of infection is the best agricultural land of the entire municipio. It is the only area of coffee production. Fewer than 1,000 people live in Yolox, but so much of the land of the municipio is unexploitable by any of the indigenous systems of agriculture that there is an acute shortage of arable land.

There is an eighth hamlet, Rancho Carrizal, in the hot, dry, northwestern area of the municipio. This is an area of subsistence farming only. It is locally distinguished for the production of several kinds of gourds employed extensively by Yoleños as drinking, eating, and storage vessels.

There are two clearly defined seasonal variations in the climate of the municipio. From June through November heavy autumnal rains fall in all the natural areas of the municipio. Precipitation diminishes in the western margin of the region. Above the hot arid lower northwest slope of Rancho Carrizal, the land is cold and semiarid. This cold semiarid northwest area is the scene of intense electrical activity which poses a danger to people and stock in the middle and upper slope areas of the municipio.

There are a number of tracks which link the principal hamlets with the centrally located pueblo. The seasonal fluctuation in rainfall occasions a great variation in the state of these trails. In the dry season they are clearly defined, though arduous. During the rainy season they are all but obliterated. These paths are steep, often stepped. Walking is the most widely used means of travel. A sierra-hardened Yoleño can walk to the most distant hamlet in five or six hours in reasonably dry weather. He could make the same journey by mule in the same time under the same circumstances. Such is the rugged nature of the terrain that no advantage in time is gained by riding in most cases. The most tenacious and intrepid motorized

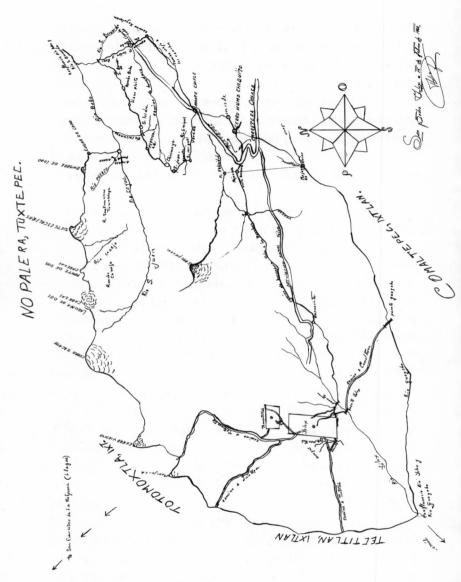

3. *San Pedro Yolox as drawn by a "son of the pueblo"*

vehicle is, of course, incapable of negotiating these trails even in the best climatic conditions.

Map 3, drawn by "a son of the pueblo," illustrates the extent and salient features of the municipio as locally viewed. The amateur cartographer had spent four years outside the village and received part of his primary education at an American mission school.

History is worrying about things which have happened and
if you are not too worried about what is happening to you
now, *you can make these fine studies.*

[B. H. J. FIELD NOTES]

A small minority of Yoleños are aware that their pueblo
has been the subject of some scholarly attention, much of
it historical. The most highly prized source of historical
data is Dr. Rosendo Pérez García's *History of the Sierra
Juárez.* A copy of the *History* is always at hand in the
Municipal Hall. All four of the village families named as
most wealthy possess copies of the Pérez work and it is
frequently mentioned and consulted by the officials of the
local government. The municipal secretary's responses
to questions about village history were largely influenced
by this volume.

You know Dr. Pérez has written about this pueblo in his book.
You know that our people came here from below. It seems that
the pueblo was ruled by a king or chief. They say two brothers
used to rule, one in the high land and the other in the low coun-

*try. Before all these things happened all the Chinantec lived
together in the lower Chinantla. The Mexicans [Aztecs] came
here in 1420. The Mexicans called the pueblo Yoloxochitlán,
which means the place of flowers. The people here had to give
gold and feathers and spears with copper tips to the Mexicans.
The first Spaniard came to the pueblo in 1599. Our pueblo was
very famous and important then. We were made the seat of the
parish, a title which we still hold, as you may know. Dr. Pérez
also says we have played our part in the struggle for independence and the revolution.*

[MUNICIPAL SECRETARY, FIELD NOTES]

As a people, however, the Chinantec of Yolox are not
history conscious.

*Most people in this pueblo don't know anything about Licen-
ciado Pérez. How many of those fine people in your school have
hands like that Mitla man, or Litos, or me? So you knew when
you touched our hands that we are not scholars. We know we
are here in this pueblo. We know our pueblo. It is the only corner of the Republic that most of us do know.*   [B. H. J. FIELD
NOTES]

The overwhelming public preoccupation centers upon
the land issue. This is a public matter which impinges
directly upon the private well-being of almost every
Yoleño family. The primary concern with the past as such
is rooted in the belief that an objective examination of it
will justify their claims to land which they have lost to
their neighbors through the interposition of state arbitration or by bloody strife. Most free discussions about
the past invariably gravitate toward the question of the
true territorial limits of the municipio.

*Some people say the people came here from China. Others say
that all the people came up here from Valle Nacional long ago*

*in a time of great sickness because the air was better here. But
for the most part, the people don't know about such things as
that. The people of this place are mostly* campesinos [*farmers*]
*and we don't think about things like that. We are very poor
and it is our misfortune to live among savage and brutal people who will not deal honestly with us as we have always dealt
with them. Those of Comaltepec are the worst of the orphans
[bastards] of this world. Have they told you how these orphans
are always trying to steal our lands?* [L. C. FIELD NOTES]

Yoleños are mountain marginals who have for most
of their history been either tributary to or directly dom-
inated by larger societies. Conflicts with other Chinantec-
speaking groups probably inspired by land disputes and
the lengthy history of Nahuatl, Spanish, and Mexican
Republican state intrusion have forced Yoleños up the
northern escarpment of the Sierra Juárez into more marginal lands and a harsher environment.

The strictures of this harsh environment have made
Yolox a community of extremely practical people con-
stantly absorbed in the vital problem of finding exploitable
agricultural terrain.

*To keep alive, to sustain those who will not eat if you die—
that is what a man must try to do here. That takes almost all
the time we have* now. *So we don't worry about any other time.
Time to come? Well, God is deciding about how that time will
be. And as for that time which has gone, it is surely gone.*
[C. H. D. FIELD NOTES]

This struggle precludes most purely speculative concern
with the past. Speculation about the origins of the highland Chinantec of Yolox is almost the exclusive concern
of clerics, historians, and linguists.

*This is a small pueblo and we are a poor people. We have never
had anything to do with these kings and men of great power.
I do not think it was ever very different, but we really do not
know—anyway, I know very little about it. Why do your people
want to know things like that anyway?*   [L. C. FIELD NOTES]

It is impossible to speak with anything like temporal
precision about the movement of the Chinantec-speaking
peoples into the Chinantla. These people either brought
with them or developed a martial tradition. The Chinantla
has long been the scene of intense intercommunal strife.
The losers in these land feuds have quite literally been
forced to the mountain wall. This period of autonomy was
ended for most of the Chinantla when it was reduced to
tributary status by the expanding Aztecan state.

The highland Chinantec name for the municipio is *NOO*
(heart). The name which was imposed by the dominant
Aztecs is *Yolox*. The municipio currently bears the name
of its Spanish-imposed patron, St. Peter, while still re-
taining the abbreviated form of its pre-Columbian Nahuatl name, *Yoloxochitlán*. For all official purposes the
municipio is known as San Pedro Yolox, but the old Chinantec name still survives.

There is a firm conviction on the part of most people
that life has always been essentially the same.

*For my part I think we have always lived as we live now. Peo-
ple always have to have a little corn or some beans to keep them
living. Those old ones who lived in those old times that everyone, even the oldest people, have forgotten, they had to eat to
live. They had to sow corn and beans and tomatoes and all those
things people eat also, even as we must now.*   [S. M. FIELD
NOTES]

24

*As it is now, so it must have been then too. It was so for our
grandfathers. And when we who are alive now are old or dead
it will be the same for our children that come after us. This is
a poor pueblo. If our grandfathers were rich and powerful,
then where is their treasure and who knows where their pal-
aces are to be found? If their times had been different, then
the people would not have forgotten those times. What kind of
a king could a poor pueblo like ours have? We are the children
of campesinos and the ones who come after us will be the
children of campesinos. We are a poor people.* [P. L. M.
FIELD NOTES]

The harsh ongoing realities of Yoleño economy preclude any serious mass interest in conventional history.
All village descriptions and the vast bulk of self-descrip-
tions invariably include allusions to poverty. Allowing
for the tendency of families to underestimate their resources to avoid the enmity of their neighbors and the
propensity to assume a position of poverty in bargaining,
poverty is a real and pervasive grim fact of Yoleño existence. Yoleño speculation about the past as such is rare
and lacks precision in the same way that their preindus-
trial concept of daily time is unspecific.

Yoleños are not a taciturn people but discussions about
history are often awkward and are likely to end unsatis-
factorily unless structured along very general lines. One
of the most serious impediments to rapport is the fear of
being thought *tonto* (ignorant). In discussions about conventional history most villagers are on uncertain ground.
If left open enough, however, almost all discussions about
history develop into autobiographies or apologies for the
Yoleño position in the running land feud between San
Pedro Yolox and the neighboring municipio of Santiago
Comaltepec. Since their low standard of living is the

primary concern of most people in the municipio, it is no
wonder that most discussions about history should gravitate toward the principal cause of their poverty, the acute
shortage of arable land.

This extreme scarcity of exploitable land has probably
been the decisive factor in the process of tribal and village
strife and fragmentation which forced the Yoleños to
the marginal mountain environment they now inhabit.
This process has precipitated the three great population
moves which are still a part of the dimly remembered
history of the inhabitants of the municipio. At some un-
determined time in their pre-Aztecan past, when the
highland Chinantec lived in autonomous communities, the
pressure of population upon arable land forced a segment
of several families to migrate to the present Santiago
Comaltepec. The initial separation appears to have been
relatively amicable. Pueblos in the region of Atepec have
a tradition of hostility to the two Yoloxes provoked by
disagreements about land. So it would appear that San
Pedro Yolox, the parent community, was actively allied
with a second Yolox, the present Santiago Comaltepec.
But as the constriction occasioned by the expansion of
larger, state-organized cultures increased, the highland
Chinantec were obliged to contend with each other for
the choice downslope terrain in their marginal environment. To the north of them were the large vigorous Chinantec lowlanders who had forced them upslope. The
Zapotecans blocked any possible southward expansion.
And the area was sealed effectively by the Mazatec on
the east and the Mixtec to the west.

In the mid-nineteenth century another segment composed of several families left the pueblo and settled in

the adjacent district of Etla. These families were left without land after a judgment handed down by Republican authority awarded the parcels they had been exploiting to Comaltepec (Pérez García 1956[1]:103). The colonists have acquired land and local dominance near Atatlauca. Their settlement is now the municipal agency of El Porvenir, sometimes called *Las Bocas*. There are amicable relations between the colonists and their original home. Except for a softly but persistently expressed conviction that their colonial cousins are a trifle lawless and quick to anger, the two groups regard themselves as one people. The critical factor in the diametrically opposed sets of relationships between the highland Chinantec of Yolox and their former *paisanos* (fellow villagers) is distance. Because the *ranchos* of Porvenir are not in competition for land with the home pueblo they have maintained cordial ties with it. Because the earlier colony, that segment which founded Comaltepec, is competing with the home pueblo from a position of numerical superiority for scarce arable terrain, these two highland Chinantec peoples are traditional foes.

It would be difficult to overestimate the centrality of this traditional controversy in the thinking of the municipio. Though paramount in the village concept of history, this bitter land feud is all too current. In 1962 the central village was occupied by an armed party from Comaltepec and during the siege many houses were damaged and persons of all ages and sexes were killed and wounded. There is a small detachment of soldiers stationed permanently in Yolox to prevent a recurrence of the fighting.

Since your eyes are closed too I will tell you that this is no grand place. You don't need eyes to know that though. Some people say we are very backward but this is my pueblo and I was born here and I have come back so that I might die here. I have seen many places but this is my pueblo. . . .

[B. P. FIELD NOTES]

San Pedro Yolox is a chain of settlement which sprawls down the steep slopes of a high broken valley of the northeastern Sierra Juárez. There are no rail connections and only the most indirect bus connections. Two times a day a second-class bus pauses briefly on the cold, windy flank of Cerro Pelón, one of the high environing peaks of the valley in which the village lies. Cerro Pelón is, in good weather, approximately a three-hour journey from the village.

Trucks transport goods ordered from Oaxaca City as far as a motor vehicle can proceed down the Ramal de Yolox (an unpaved spur of the Oaxaca-Tuxtepec paved road). This point varies with the state of the dirt road. Under the most favorable conditions, however, it is necessary to transfer cargo from motorized to animal or human carriers arduous miles from the village. Vast quantities of goods by local standards are moved great distances into and out of the village by the traditional Mexican style of head carrying.

This tenuous, indirect road-linkage and the one telegraph-telephone of the municipio, located in one of the stores of the village, are the only village contacts with the district seat at Ixtlán de Juárez and with the state capital at Oaxaca City. In 1915 the telephone-telegraph line was destroyed as a consequence of the revolutionary hostilities. The service was not restored until 1956. In that year the judicial secretary was trained in the operation of this facility. He sends a dozen communications a month on the average and receives approximately twice that number. The storekeepers, the village priest, and the members of the garrison are the primary users of the telegraph. It does not appear that any but the wealthiest families of the village use the telephone, and then it is only employed for the most urgent official and commercial purposes.

There is no way out of the village except up and there is no way to reach it save a taxing descent. From the bleak uninhabited crossroads and bus stop of Cerro Pelón the Ramal de Yolox descends the slopes of the mountain to where it joins a tract known locally as *La Vereda*. The Vereda is the main route of entrance and egress. This trail clings precariously to the forested slopes of Cerro Pelón. For much of its upper extent it is nothing more than a narrow, steeply inclined shelf between the overhanging summit and the formidable *barrancas*, or deep chasms, common in this region. As it spirals precipitously downslope, the main track crosses several streams. From late November or early December these watercourses are dry, low, or, at any rate, contained within their banks through May. But from early June through October and often later the rains convert them into roaring torrents which often leave their banks. The more formidable of these swift creeks are spanned by log bridges which are often submerged or even washed away in the rainy season. Immediately before entering the lowest link of the chain of habitation, the route crosses the only board bridge along its length. This span has also been carried away at least once within the memory of many villagers. Beyond the bridge the trail inclines sharply upward, terminating at the foot of one of the main streets of the village.

Street nomenclature is partially indicative of the main historical influences upon the village. All streets and dwellings have names and numbers assigned to them by the government of Mexico. These names are commemorative of salient dates, main concepts and dominant personages in Mexican history generally and more particularly in Republican history. The three largest

The traditional Mexican style of head carrying.

stores of the village are located respectively at numbers 1, 2, and 3 Avenida de la Independencia. There is a gentleman who rents mules and runs a small store at number 14 Avenida Nacional. There is a still smaller shop at number 25 on the same street. A *curandero* and diviner lives on Calle Porfirio Díaz and many of the soldiers of the small detachment now garrisoning the village take their meals at number 1 Avenida Benito Juárez. This is the only house in the village where meals may be purchased. The leader of the village band and cantor lives on a steep path in the upper part of the village known variously as Calle Norte, Calle Progreso or Avenida de Progreso.

The old Chinantec designations for the principal paths of the village are still remembered. Thus Avenida Nacional is also spoken of as *FUHMI'IH*, the path to Valle Nacional, and Calle Norte, or Avenida de Progreso, is remembered as *MI NAH'A*, or the path which leads to a flat place.

Mail is addressed to San Pedro Yolox, generally via Ixtlán de Juárez without regard to any specific address. ·Correspondence is collected at the district Post Office and brought to the Municipal Hall where it is retrieved by the villagers. This service is very sporadic. Its quality fluctuates with the degree of diligence and sobriety of the policeman dispatched by the municipal Authority.

While Chinantec and Spanish street designations coexist, villagers say that the numerical designation of house sites is new. There does not appear to be any consistency in the enumeration of dwellings. Most villagers regard street designations of any kind extremely lightly. Many do not know either the number of their house or the name of the street on which it is situated.

The village streets are universally narrow, rutted, unpaved, meandering paths between the several clusters of house sites which make up the village. The links of this chain of habitation vary in size and accessibility with the contour of the rugged slopes to which they cling. For all its occasional and dispersed appearance, San Pedro is as centralized as the terrain permits. The traditional central plaza is absent but the village is constructed roughly in a relationship of linear centrality above and below the church.

Two of the four stores of the village and all public buildings, the Municipal Hall, the residence of the priest, the residence of the three Zapotecan schoolteachers and the school are all downslope from the church. The lower village is often spoken of as *el centro*. Persons living in the rockier, colder, less verdant upper portions of the village speak wistfully of their remoteness from the "center." They regret especially their inability to hear the recordings played for the diversion of the pueblo during fiestas over the loud-speaker.

A small municipally owned electric plant supplies power intermittently to the Municipal Hall, the rectory, the Health Center, and the school. The principal sources of illumination are pine torches, *gandiles* (fuel oil burning lanterns fashioned of beer cans), and candles. Next to electricity, utilized by a very small minority of villagers, candles are the preferred means of illumination but their cost obliges most families to use them very sparingly.

The principal public source of water, *el chorro*, is a clear spring which gushes from the mountainside in four separate streams. Two of the streams, separated from the general chorro area by a board fence, are used as shower baths. The other two streams supply water for the concrete laundry basins nearby and fill the odd assortment of tin cans, clay pots, and drinking gourds which supply general domestic needs. Families in the more remote areas of the village take their water from local sources whenever possible. But many of these local sources are dry from January through May, obliging distant householders to supply their domestic needs from the central supply. El chorro is no mere center of domestic drudgery. Village housewives take a leisurely approach to laundering and there is generally much washing of hair, bathing of babies, and exchanging of hearsay. The trail to *el monte,* the commons from which most village families

El chorro *is no mere center of domestic drudgery.*

obtain kindling, passes the chorro. Village children bound to and from the common wood lot pause to play and exchange greetings as their mothers make a show of scrubbing an already thrice-scrubbed garment and the last bit of gossip is shared.

Houses are occasionally adjoining and more rarely even attached. But the majority of the 130 house sites listed in the official municipal census are situated upon plots large enough to put considerable distance between any given householder and his neighbor. Some houses are clustered in a hollow while others are perched together on an isolated slope. This clustering appears to have engendered very little in the way of the formation of factions. Some families living in the upper part of the village resist certain schemes for village improvement. The most frequent reason cited for this opposition is the fear that they will be taxed either in labor or money to initiate some innovation which will benefit the center, that is, the lower village.

In addition to the main dwelling, house sites frequently have a less substantial structure in which fowl are kept and kindling stored. A considerable portion of most house plots is given over to cultivation. *Milpas* (cornfields), cane patches, and gardens in which vegetables and herbs are grown for use as condiments or medicinal purposes are common.

With but two exceptions, namely the wealthiest of the storekeepers and the priest, all families in San Pedro Yolox are housed in one or another of the indigenous house types. Of the two indigenous house types—the adobe, or sundried brick house, and the *jacal,* or house constructed of pine or banana bark, of corn stalks, or of banana or palm leaves—adobe predominates in the village.

Several men of wide experience as housebuilders report that most adobe houses in the village consist of one room 8 meters long by about 5.5 meters wide. A portion of one wall serves as the rear base of the hearth. The cooking surface is sometimes elevated upon a crude board table covered with adobe. Generally, however, the cooking area is simply a portion of the hard-packed earthen floor. Such dwellings commonly have a single door of pine planking and one small, square window. There is no chimney and the hearth smoke issues through these openings. Food and farm implements and other household items not in immediate use are stored in the *tapanco,* a space between the ceiling rafters and the roof. This space is reached by means of a log ladder. The hard-packed earthen floor is the sleeping area. Beds are rarely used. Palm sleeping mats are generally used, although the poorest families often employ flattened, cast-off cardboard boxes for this purpose. No Yoleño house, not even the most elegant, can boast of plumbing. The sheltered latrine is a rarity and with but few exceptions families employ designated portions of their house plots as latrine areas.

Household shrines are all but universal in the village. They vary in form from a simple pine plank suspended from the ceiling rafters with pictures of saints upon it to elaborate altars adorned with images purchased in Oaxaca City. A portion of a wall may be covered with pictures of saints but the most common arrangement is to employ a table as an altar. Christ crucified, the Virgins of Ocotlán and Juquila, St. Martín de Porres and St. Anthony are most frequently represented. *Estampas,* or holy pictures, are sold in three stores of the village. Altar tables often serve a dual purpose as they are sometimes pressed into domestic use.

The inventory of domestic essentials for a village household consists in the main of *petates* (palm sleeping mats) ; low stools and chairs of domestic manufacture; clay pots purchased or bartered for in Quiotepec or brought in from Oaxaca City; clay dishes and pitchers from Quiotepec or Oaxaca City; cargo nets of varying size purchased in the stores of the village; several kinds of eating, drinking, and storage vessels fashioned from gourds, generally by the individual family; a number of kinds of woven baskets of local and Oaxaca City manufacture; a *metate* (grinding stone) purchased in the stores of the village for grinding corn; and *comales,* or clay griddles.

The villagers make a number of living units which are all referred to as jacales. The distribution of the several kinds of jacal appears to be determined by the type of building material available. Palm-thatch, banana-leaf, and banana-bark houses are found only in the hot humid northeastern hamlets where the tropical flora provides such building materials in abundance.

Cane-stalk houses are found both in the village and the low-lying hamlets, but they are more numerous in the dependent hamlets, because the tropical climate of that portion of the municipio renders them more practical and because there is a greater abundance of cane there. Houses of pine slats and houses of pine bark are found only in the village and the upper region of the municipio. Such houses are generally about 5 meters in length and about 3.5 meters in width. Corn-stalk houses are found in both the seven hot wet hamlets and the hot dry rancho, *Carrizal,* but not in the central village.

Nails purchased in the stores of the village are used in the construction of pine-slat and pine-bark houses. Cane-stalk, banana-bark, banana-leaf, and corn-stalk houses—the dominant house types of the hot wet hamlets—are lashed with a tough tying vine called *majagua*.

The type of dwelling occupied by any given family is very largely determined by its economic circumstances. The poorest families live in the least substantial jacales: houses of corn stalks, houses of banana leaves and houses of banana bark. Informants agreed that the first two types should be rebuilt after a single year of occupancy under normal weather conditions. Houses of banana bark are said to have a life span of two years. Pine-slat houses are said to last approximately ten years while a house of cane leaves in reasonable repair was pointed out which had been constructed thirteen years ago. Palm houses are the most durable of the hamlet house types, often remaining livable for as long as twenty years. Adobe is the preferred form in the village, but economic circumstances sometimes oblige families to modify this form. There are a number of adobe houses with one or more pine-plank walls.

Two storekeepers employ sheet aluminum as a roofing material. A portion of the school and the latrine area of the Municipal Hall are also roofed with the same material. Only one man, the brother of the wealthiest storekeeper of the village, employs sheet aluminum as a roofing material in the hamlets. He lives in the only concrete house in all that portion of the municipio. For the most part, however, villagers employ rough tiles for this purpose.

Still another new building material has been recently introduced with somewhat less customer satisfaction. A factory based in Oaxaca City produced and distributed by means of one of the storekeepers of the village *ojas de cartón,* sheet cardboard. Taking pains to expound its merits in the dry season, the distributor convinced a number of families to purchase it as house construction material. These heavy cardboard sheets were available in three attractive speculator colors, red, black and green, at 7.5 pesos per sheet.

Because they never leave here some of my poor paisanos *believed the new carton would last as long as the merchants swore that it would. When they found out the truth, they became very angry and wanted to knock down those new houses. You know, a man would need about 400 of those* ojas de cartón *for a small house. That would cost three thousand* pesos *for that cardboard alone!* *   [P. L. F. FIELD NOTES]

The largest piece of flat village terrain is the site of the church and its grounds. The open courtyard between the church and the priest's residence is the scene of much public interaction. Fiesta celebrations, volleyball games, piñata parties and fireworks displays all take place in this centrally located *atrio.* The municipal Authority, noting with disapproval the rather dubious claim to sacredness of some of this activity, drew the following nice but functional distinction: any group relying upon strong drink for the facilitation of its proceedings must not gather in the church. As a result of this pronouncement, the adjoining sacristy is in great demand as an informal meeting place for the men of the village. The outdoor speaker of

---

* Three thousand pesos is a sum sufficient to maintain a village family of four persons for a year or more. Indeed, there are families of twice that size whose actual annual expenditures are less than that amount.

the public address system is mounted on a pole at the edge of the courtyard. Over this public apparatus members of the village Authority issue announcements in the public interest, acknowledge birthdays, and play, and play again the half dozen or so recordings purchased at public expense for the diversion of the "sons of the pueblo."

The long three-roomed adobe school stands just above the rectory on a smaller piece of relatively flat ground. By day the six sexually segregated grades fill or half fill the three classrooms. Attendance mirrors the marginality of life in the village and the constant transhumance necessary to sustain most families even at this level. Children of the minority of village families making the sacrifice involved in maintaining a child in the high pueblo attend sporadically. The range in subsistence level is reflected in the age spread of any class. There are pubescent children in all six grades. The age spread of the first grade is from six through twelve years. The ten-year-old son of one of the shopkeepers is completing the fourth grade while the fifteen-year-old son of a campesino is in the third grade.

At night the school is often pressed into service as a civic center. Then, seated on the same wooden benches occupied earlier by their children, village adults, generally men, install their Authority, debate public questions and celebrate the day of National Independence. The school committee gives an early autumn feast of new maize on the long porch which runs the length of the school and there is just enough level ground for the basketball game between the married and the single men which is the climax of the *Fiesta Patria* (Independence Day) festivities.

The formal administrative center for the village and its dependent localities is a long, narrow adobe building generally called *el municipio*. Most of this structure has been preempted as a barracks area for the 14 federal soldiers and their families stationed in Yolox to prevent further hostility between the villagers and their traditional enemies from Comaltepec.

The Municipal Hall doubles as a reception center for the occasional prestigious visitor, august court, executive chamber and men's club to the twenty-four married sons of the pueblo who constitute the village government. Their *casquillos*, ceremonial rods of office, line one of the walls. The president's Carnival mask hangs on another wall just above the highly esteemed municipal typewriter. The personnel of the municipal orchestra gather there to rehearse the airs of Carnival and those charged with public office and their friends convene impromptu assemblies to convert the cash accruing from certain fines into strong drink.

El centro de salud, the Health Center recently constructed by the villagers with federal assistance, is the most nonindigenous structure in the entire pueblo. A nurse is stationed in this little concrete, aluminum-roofed field infirmary by the National Campaign against Onchocerciasis. Sewing machines are available for the instruction of village women and proper playground swings of Oaxaca City manufacture sway incongruously and generally unused in the precious flat ground in front of it.

*Maize is what is important because you have to eat in order
to live. . . . The real money for buying maize comes from the
sale of coffee. You see, there are a lot of poor people here
who do not have enough maize to last them all through the
year. Now when their maize runs out they have to buy more
with the money they get from selling a little coffee.*

[H. P. FIELD NOTES]

Most village households are directly dependent upon subsistence agriculture. Even among that small prestigious
fraction of village families deriving a significant part of
their living from commercial activity, this dependence
upon the land is merely diminished and not minimized.
Indeed, the prestige which these families enjoy is in no
small part a consequence of their having augmented their
landholdings by their nonagricultural enterprises.*

* A small (5.3 percent) number of households invest all or significant fractions of their time and labor in lucrative subsistence activities not directly connected with agriculture. Three men devote the
bulk of their time to the management of full-time, year-round
stores in the village. One man operates a smaller seasonal shop
there also. There is one full-time storekeeper in the hot wet hamlets

Arable land is the principal kind of security pledged by men to secure loans from their *Barrio* Association (semilocalized sodality) or from one of the merchants. Land even more than draft animals is the most valued possession of a household.

When villagers describe their land as being very ugly, they are lamenting the relative scarcity of agriculturally exploitable terrain in their municipio. The municipal president and the judicial secretary, both subsistence farmers, were in accord with the estimate of Pérez García (1956[I]:102–3) that fully nine-tenths of the land area of the municipio is inexploitable by any of the locally employed agrarian technologies. No village farmer took issue with this estimate.

Villagers employ both fire and plow agriculture. Swiddenage is the universal form in the hot humid northeastern onchocerciasis-infected ranchos, while both fire and plow agriculture are practiced in the temperate or cold forested upper slope areas of the municipio and in Rancho Carrizal. Plow agriculture is the dominant method in the region of the ceremonial pueblo itself, in the lower mar-

and six village men who are part-time tenders of seasonal stores or occasional peddlers catering to the needs of villagers engaged in agricultural activity outside the High Village. Just as the highly prestigious status of *comerciante*, or merchant, is accorded to only four of the householders engaged in storekeeping or peddling, only one of the five Yoleño women who bake bread for sale is known as *la panadera*, **the** baker. The baker makes bread two or three times a week and runs the only place in the village where meals are sold. The other women engaged in baking make bread primarily for sale during fiestas and bake only occasionally at other times. There is one butcher who slaughters most from October to May but who is totally unemployed at his trade only during the month of August. There is a recurrent, occasional demand for candlemaking, carpentry, cane milling and lime slaking. Only one of the four householders who rent mules and horses can be said to conduct a year-round livery stable.

gins of the cold forested upper slope region and in the hot dry rancho of Carrizal.

All kinds of agricultural labor with the exception of sowing are male tasks. The traditional division of labor which places women in the house and men in the fields is only an approximated ideal. Women in the poorest families or widowed women whose male kin have married into distant families or left the municipio are obliged to do field labor.

Just as most householders possess title to their house sites, so most also possess one or more small plots of land, very often located in differing regions of the municipio. Plots belonging to families in poor to moderately poor circumstances vary from 1 to 1.5 hectares. The wealthiest village families may hold plots of 5 and even 6 hectares. People say they received their plots as an inheritance from their ancestors who "made the pueblo." In the representative reflections of a blind *anciano:* "mostly everyone has his own inheritance, but there are some who have none, and if they have none, then well, then they have nothing!" (H. P. Field Notes.) Apart from private

The traditional division of labor which places women in the house and men in the fields is only an approximated ideal.

tenure there is only one of the three common forms of Mexican tenure in Yolox. There are no *ejido* plots* in the municipio and many farmers had only the haziest notion of the ejido concept and some had never heard of it at all.

Customary usage assures every "son of the pueblo" the right to petition the Authority for permission to *"tumbar un monte,"* that is, the formal assent of the pueblo to clear and exploit a portion of the common lands. A respectful oral petition is made before either the president or the entire Authority for the right to clear and cultivate a specific parcel of the communal lands. The Authority as a whole grants or denies the petition. The need and diligence of the petitioner, which are generally public knowledge long before he states his case, are prime factors in the ruling.

Plot size is locally determined by the fraction or multiple of a standard measure of seed, an *almud* (4 kilos), which is required to sow a given parcel. An almud of seed will sow approximately 1 hectare. A friend and informant confided that he owned three plots: one in his rancho of three-fourths almud, and two in the vicinity of the high pueblo of one almud and three-fourths almudes respectively. Thus this subsistence farmer maintains his family of ten persons in characteristic Yoleño marginality on 2.5 hectares of land.

The verb *confide* is all too inadequate an indicator of the intimacy of amity which must be established before a man will speak of his land. An elderly blind informant who was interviewed about the appropriateness of questions about private tenure expressed the prevailing atti-

* Federally owned plots exploited by particular families.

tude in this crisp and accurate prediction: "What! Ask a man about his *parcelas* (parcels [of land]) ? You might as well ask him what goes on on his sleeping mat at night! Unless he's your friend he's bound to lie to you!" (B. P. Field Notes.)

Maize is the mainstay of the village diet. Maize is "real food" and improves the flavor of many other foods of doubtful propriety. The flesh of the fox, because it is said to bear a disturbing similarity to the dog or the coyote, and the flesh of the monkey, because the sexual organs of that animal are said to be extremely humanoid, are very low prestige foods, ranking even below wild greens. A number of informants admitted to having been tricked into eating *moles* (fricassees) made of this low prestige meat. In all cases they attributed their deception to the fact that their deceivers had added *nixtamal,* maize dough, to the noxious dish, thus changing its flavor to something like that of the squirrel, which is extensively consumed.

The value of agricultural land depends very largely upon its maize yield. The hot humid northeastern lower slope is known generally as *tierra buena.* The reason most often advanced for this appellation is that this land yields *tonamil,* a second smaller maize crop which is sown in late autumn and harvested in June. The first maize crop in this hot humid tierra buena is sown in late spring and gathered in early autumn. In this initial maize planting small pumpkin and a kind of string bean are sown together. Another kind of bean known locally as *delgado* is sown in the same furrow but halfway between the mounds in which maize, pumpkin and *ejotes* (string beans) have been planted.

The hot humid tierra buena is also the area of cultivation of coffee, the only important cash crop of the municipio. Most families own some trees and those who do not arrange to cut for or with their more fortunate neighbors on shares. Cane for local use as *panela* (loaf sugar) and the manufacture of a potent crude rum called *chingare* is cultivated most extensively in this region. Fig, avocado, mango, and several kinds of citrus and banana are the most important food-producing trees which grow in this area. There also *majagua* and *bejuco*, the tying vines vital in house lashing and basketry, are principally found.

In the hot dry Carrizal area there is only one maize crop. The inhabitants of this area are the last to begin agricultural activity because of the late arrival of the rains. It is often mid to late summer before the earth is sufficiently moist to cultivate. Some cane is grown in Carrizal and it is the only part of the municipio where *maguey*, the cactus from which mescal, that strong, indispensable alcoholic accompaniment of virtually every fiesta and crisis rite, is distilled.

Carrizal is locally distinguished for the production of a very large kind of mango and gourds vital for the manufacture of household drinking, eating, and storage vessels. The wealthiest man in the village possesses land in Carrizal and does resort to artificial irrigation. Diligent inquiry failed to disclose any other instance of artificial irrigation.

The remaining portion of the municipio, the temperate to cold slopes and broken valley floor environing the pueblo itself and the higher, colder mountains which extend to the southwest of it, yield a single maize crop annually. Upland sowing is generally done in early March and the crop is gathered in early November. A spindly cane is grown as high as the pueblo. Apple, peach, *anona* (custard apple), fig, and walnut trees also are found at this level.

The foregoing is a description of the most general agricultural regime but there is wide variance in the particular subsistence activities of individual families. A few people may try to get a second crop near the pueblo; some burn first, others plant immediately after the first harvest. Some farmers intercrop and some do not. "Every man does what he can to make a crop" (P. L. F. Field Notes).

Household subsistence activity is necessarily bound up with the performance of field labor on plots located at different altitudes and widely varying ecological zones. Most household subsistence units sow their upslope parcels some time in March. In May they are obliged to descend to the hot humid rancho to sow their downslope plots. By June the necessity to weed their upslope milpas compels most household heads to shift residence once more. By July or August the downslope parcels require weeding. In October the downslope fields which were sown in May must be harvested. By All Saints' Day or in early November they must ascend to the upslope fields to gather the maize which was sown in March. By December tonamil, the second downslope corn crop, must be sown. Add to this simplest regime the general reliance upon both slash and burn and plow agriculture in land which must be prepared for sowing at differing times and under widely varying conditions and some notion of the intensity and complexity of that microtranshumance which is an imperative of village subsistence can be deduced.

The quality of village subsistence is profoundly seasonal. The relative absence of extreme hunger is directly linked with the differing maturation rates of the staples of village diet.

There is generally laughter when you ask the people how many times they eat in a day. The laughter is born of shame because sometimes we don't eat at all and sometimes we eat four times a day. The truth is we eat when there is something to eat! In harvest time, sure, we eat three times a day, but in August we do well to eat once a day for food is very scarce then. August is the month in which we eat less, for at no other time is maize so scarce.   [L. C. FIELD NOTES]

Many persons informed me in strictest confidence that their families were often obliged to fast for one or two days a week during the month of August. Villagers tend to state their dietary preferences as follows: food which men may eat under conditions of extreme hunger, ordinary fare and high prestige fiesta food. There is a lowest prestige stress diet which may be consumed under conditions of hunger, sickness, or a period of strife which might oblige the Chinantec to quit their village for traditional refuge in the fastnesses of their environing sierra. "Then a man might have to eat nothing but wild greens, monkey, fox and even coyote!" The fact that significant numbers of Yoleños regularly incorporate all of these lowest prestige foods except the most loathsome coyote into their household dietary regime is graphic evidence of the acute hunger which is a regular factor in the lives of many villagers.

Maize and a variety of green and dried beans are the staples of conventional fare. However, many of the poorest families consider beans to be fiesta fare and do not eat them as often as do their more fortunate neighbors.

Rice, chocolate, eggs, milk, fresh bread and moles made of beef, pork, chicken or turkey are the most often mentioned highest prestige fiesta foods. Most villagers were emphatic in stating that these were foods which most people would never expect to have *enough* of. Everyone is, of course, aware of the existence of these things. These are the foods which villagers themselves would eat under optimum circumstances. They are the foods which villagers would serve important people from Mexico City and the staples of good dream diets. In actual practice, however, most villagers count themselves lucky to be able to secure a 2 or 4 peso bit of beef or pork with which to make a stew. Table 1 illustrates the complexity of the general agricultural regime related to the principal village-wide fiestas and the seasonal fluctuation in the price of the staples of village diet.

Despite the relative remoteness of the municipio, money plays an appreciable part in household economy. The four stores of the village supply a number of household necessities; yard goods and clothing, shoes and *huaraches* and soles of rubber and leather, candles, pitchpine and fuel oil for illumination, soap, salt, patent medicines, cooking oil, clay griddles and pots form only a partial inventory of items which a household cannot provide through domestic manufacture.

All but the most marginal household subsistence aggregates are occasionally obliged to employ their neighbors for brief periods. Public service, major participation in the *mayordomía* system (administration of the fiesta cycle), the incapacity of an adult family member or, in a minority of cases, the requirements of other lucrative subsistence activities often impose the most imperative need for such assistance. The most intense demand for extra household labor occurs at harvest time when a household subsistence team may be augmented by from one to as many as thirty field laborers. If a somewhat less marginal family has contracted for extra field labor, or if the wife of such a family is especially incapacitated by the ultimate stages and immediate aftermath of pregnancy, some women from more marginal families are hired to feed the additional workers or spell the pregnant woman at the metate.

Households of differing wealth levels are often linked by a system of cooperative joint enterprise known locally as *compania*. The companía system links a disadvantaged *compañero*, or caretaker, with a wealthier *dueño*, or owner in a partnership of mutual advantage. There appears to be the most direct correlation between companía relationships and less casual kinds of *compadrazgo* (ritual, fictive kinship) ties. A godchild may obtain capital from his godfather of marriage for the purchase of barnyard fowl, a pig, or even a yoke of oxen. The compañero tends the stock for a specified period and then it is slaughtered or sold in the presence of both parties. The profits above the original capital investment of the dueño are shared equally between dueño and compañero. Companía relationships are mutually advantageous. Compañeros have the use of the stock they feed and tend. If there is no stipulation to the contrary they may rent it to persons wishing to contract for the use of draft animals. Dueños

Table 1: *Subsistence and ceremonial cycles related to food prices*

| | AGRICULTURAL CYCLE | | | | FOOD PRICES (FOR 4 KILOS) | | | |
| | HIGH VILLAGE | | RANCHOS* | | | | | FIESTAS** |
	PLOW	HOE	TEMPORAL	TONAMIL	CORN	BEANS	PEPPERS	
January	—	Harvest corn	—	Cultivate	3.20	12.00	7.00	Discípula, 15th
February	2d plowing	—	—	Cultivate	3.20	12.00	7.00	Carnival
March	3d plowing; sow corn and string beans	Sow corn and beans	—	—	3.20	12.00	7.00	—
April	Sow black beans	—	Slash; burn	—	4.00	12.00	7.00	Holy Week
May	Harvest pumpkins; cultivate	Cultivate	Sow corn and string beans	—	5.00	12.00	7.00	—
June	Harvest pumpkins; cultivate	Cultivate	—	Harvest corn	5.50	12.00	7.00	St. Peter, 29th

Month							
July	—	Slash; burn	Sow beans; cultivate	—	5.50	12.00	7.00	—
August	Harvest black beans	Harvest beans	Harvest peppers; cultivate	—	6.50	12.00	7.00	Ocotlán, 15th
September	—	—	—	—	6.50	12.00	4.00	Independence, 16th
October	Harvest corn and string beans	—	Harvest corn and string beans	Slash	3.20	12.00	4.00	—
November	—	—	—	Burn	3.20	12.00	7.00	All Souls, 1st–2d
December	1st plowing	—	Harvest black beans	Sow corn	3.20	12.00	7.00	Christmas, 25th

* Cycle begins somewhat later in Rancho Carrizal.
** Those attended most widely.

are certain of receiving at least their original investment in the stock. They may repossess the stock upon the death of the compañero. There is a probability that they will receive at least a modest profit upon the expiration of the compañía agreement. During the term of the accord they are not responsible for tending or feeding the stock. Dueños appear to come largely from households with title to good crop land from which they derive much of the capital they invest. Stock is free ranging from November through early March but must be corralled and fed for the remainder of the year. Thus a compañía frees the wealthier dueño from the necessity of investing time, labor and capital in the tending and feeding of stock which he can spend more profitably on his crop lands or in some commercial enterprise. The compañero, quite apart from the use of the animals involved, is assured a greater measure of protection from the clandestine malicious damage which villagers often resort to.

You see the face but you cannot know the heart. If a man has it in for me, he won't come to me and say look here paisano, *this thing or that thing you have done displeases me—no, he will give me soft words and pleasant looks and wait his turn to break something of mine or harm my animals.*

[P. L. F. FIELD NOTES]

This sharp, invidious distinction between *"nosotros,"* the members and allies of any given household, and *"otra gente,"* all other villagers, appeared to be universal. A compañía agreement is evidence that a compañero can rely upon the support of a man of consequence who might carry the matter to the Authority or even Ixtlán if he were to suffer any loss occasioned by the malice of his neighbors.

Villagers are keenly, more often than not, self-consciously, aware of the extreme marginality of their pueblo. The stark poverty of the community and the penury of most of its citizens were dominant themes in the remarks of official welcome made by the ranking members of the Authority.

This is certainly not Oaxaca City or New York! We are only a poor pueblo. We are all very glad you have chosen our humble pueblo for your scholarly work. As yet we do not know each other, but I am certain we shall get to know each other better. You will get to know us and we will get to know you and our fleas will soon get to know both of us! You have already walked over much of it so you know that our land is very ugly and that we must work very hard to pull bread from among these stumps and stones! We have very few of those comforts and grand luxuries you find in bigger, richer places in the Republic, but what we have is yours to command!

[M. L. FIELD NOTES]

Allowing for the general tendency of peasants to plead poverty and avoid wealth display for fear of provoking the envy or malice of their neighbors (Foster 1962:51–55; Lewis 1960:36; Wolf 1962:228), the most cursory observation reveals the prevalence of an extremely low standard of living for most Yoleños.

All adult persons questioned specifically concerning the village standard of living made the most direct equation between the satisfaction of hunger and an adequate standard of living. The rich are quite literally "those who eat well." Conversely, the most marginal are spoken of as "those who never eat well." Eating well is defined as the ingestion of enough of the staples to "silence the belly most of the time."

The village subsistence level is generally conceived of as a relatively unalterable continuum subdivided into three ill-defined, often overlapping, segments. A numerically insignificant number of families are said to "have enough." The great majority of village families are designated as "poor" while a sizable minority of families are said to "have nothing."

A strong element of the problematical is apparent in all discussions about the village living standard. *"Si tenemos, comemos"* ("If we have it, we eat") was the stock phrase in the responses of most poor and very poor people. Sufficiency is the standard by which villagers measure the subsistence level of a given family. The wealthiest man in the village just has a great deal more of what the poor majority and the poorest minority of his neighbors require and desire. The most marginal person, an elderly woman who had outlived all her kin and was no longer able to make the taxing ascents and descents to and from the ranchos, tearfully described the meal she would serve if she were able. On the afternoon of the same day the wealthiest man of the pueblo served a meal which was, dish for dish, the double of that feast poor Rosa could not provide. The wealthiest villager estimates his daily household expenditures at 50 pesos. Rosa estimates her annual expenditures at 48 pesos. The wide range in estimated expenditures shown in Table 2 reflects actual variation in subsistence level. As villagers are not in the habit of keeping per diem records of their expenses, their estimates are, of course, approximations. The 2.68 peso per

Table 2: *Estimated food costs of fifty-two families (25.12 percent of total 207 families)*

NO. PERSONS IN FAMILY	YEARLY EXPENSES IN PESOS	DAILY EXPENSES IN PESOS	DAILY EXPENSES PER PERSON	AVERAGE DAILY EXPENSES PER PERSON
1	48.00	.13	.13	.13
2	1,825.00	5.00	2.50	4.13
	1,825.00	5.00	2.50	
	2,920.00	8.00	4.00	
	5,475.00	15.00	7.50	
3	1,825.00	5.00	1.67	3.67
	1,825.00	5.00	1.67	
	3,650.00	10.00	3.33	
	5,475.00	15.00	5.00	
	7,300.00	20.00	6.67	
4	146.00	.40	.10	3.17
	3,650.00	10.00	2.50	
	3,650.00	10.00	2.50	
	3,650.00	10.00	2.50	
	5,475.00	15.00	3.75	
	5,840.00	16.00	4.00	
	7,300.00	20.00	5.00	
	7,300.00	20.00	5.00	
5	912.50	2.50	.50	2.30
	1,825.00	5.00	1.00	
	3,900.00	10.68	2.14	
	5,000.00	13.70	2.74	
	5,475.00	15.00	3.00	
	5,475.00	15.00	3.00	
	5,475.00	15.00	3.00	
	5,475.00	15.00	3.00	

Table 2 (*Continued*)

NO. PERSONS IN FAMILY	YEARLY EXPENSES IN PESOS	DAILY EXPENSES IN PESOS	DAILY EXPENSES PER PERSON	AVERAGE DAILY EXPENSES PER PERSON
6	450.00	1.23	.20	2.36
	500.00	1.37	.23	
	5,475.00	15.00	2.50	
	5,475.00	15.00	2.50	
	5,475.00	15.00	2.50	
	5,475.00	15.00	2.50	
	5,475.00	15.00	2.50	
	5,840.00	16.00	2.67	
	6,205.00	17.00	2.83	
	7,300.00	20.00	3.33	
	9,125.00	25.00	4.17	
7	2,190.00	6.00	.86	3.04
	4,380.00	12.00	1.71	
	5,475.00	15.00	2.14	
	5,475.00	15.00	2.14	
	7,665.00	21.00	3.00	
	10,950.00	30.00	4.29	
	18,250.00	50.00	7.14	
8	2,920.00	8.00	1.00	1.52
	3,000.00	8.22	1.03	
	4,500.00	12.33	1.54	
	7,300.00	20.00	2.50	
9	3,000.00	8.22	.91	2.40
	12,775.00	35.00	3.89	
13	5,475.00	15.00	1.15	1.15
19	9,125.00	25.00	1.32	1.32

OVER-ALL AVERAGE PER DIEM
EXPENDITURES PER PERSON   2.68

diem expenditure per person derived from Table 2 is somewhat in excess of the general average for most village families, because the sample from which the table was drawn includes the wealthiest families living in the High Village.

A rich man takes shelter behind the strong walls of his treasure. And he can say no as often as yes. And he has beasts of four feet and beasts of two feet to sweat for him. And only God Himself can say to him "go here or go there." But how many are the children of such happy fathers or can wrench so much from those who have so little. Except a man be rich he must obey. He must obey his pueblo. He must obey his socio. He must obey his father and must do the will of God. This life is a jail, and we are warders one to another.

[P. L. A. FIELD NOTES]

This expression of the powerlessness of the great mass of men before God and the fortune-favored is one of the universal aspects of the thinking of villagers about *this* world. Men especially value the good opinion of their fellows which comes with the distinction which derives from successful service. But as praise is regarded as being indissolubly alloyed by blame, prudence dictates a general avoidance of public distinction.

Local administrative and judicial authority is vested in a twenty-four-man council generally referred to quite

literally as "the Authority." *Contribuyentes,* male heads
of families who contribute toward the cost of village fiestas, choose the personnel for this governmental body from
among their number. This election is a classic example
of the office seeking the man. The sons of the pueblo,
upon the advice of those old men "ripe in judgment,"
called *ancianos* or *principales,* confer upon twenty-four
men the often pyrrhic privilege of serving their pueblo.
This distinction is, in many cases, quite literally thrust
upon them as all members serve without salary. While
the proceeds from certain *multas,* or fines, may be used
to provide drink for the body as a whole, there is no
regular remuneration for any given member.

A man's willingness to serve his pueblo in this capacity
is qualified primarily by his particular economic circumstances. Those few heads of families who are wealthy by
local standards or whose circumstances are somewhat less
marginal generally welcome this election without reservation. The vast majority of eligible persons, however, regard the mandate of their paisanos with understandable
ambivalence.

There is a general belief that the individual is obligated
to serve his pueblo. Such service is regarded as a necessary prerequisite to full adult status for males. The weight
of public censure is certain to rest heavily upon any who
disregard the will of all the sons of the pueblo. To do so
for any but the most allowable circumstances is to incur
the enmity of the collectivity. An outright refusal to serve
would oblige another man to accept the rigorous obligation. Given the hard realities of subsistence, the economic
circumstances of the man who is finally compelled to fill
the position are likely to be fully as dire as those of the

man who declined to serve. Thus, a man's outright refusal to serve occasions manifold privations for another man and his kin who are more than likely to take it hard and miss no opportunity to return the favor.

An individual who acquires a reputation as one "who does not like to obey" eventually earns its attendant negative epithet of *picaro*. In Yoleño usage a pícaro is one whose willfulness makes him difficult to integrate into his family, his barrio, and his pueblo. Compliance is a necessary element in the consensus and surface amity which are vital to the functioning of these three institutions. The repeated assumption of a posture of personal dissent puts in peril an individual's status as a family member, a son of his barrio and a son of his pueblo.

For all its attendant economic disadvantages, it cannot be denied that public service in a community which some have seen fit to characterize as drab and uninteresting (Cline 1956:635; Ford 1948:295–97) in its daily round has its congenial aspects. Upon his first encounter with the Honorable Authority, the author presented mescal and beer was presented to him. As the evening wore on there was a clearly discernible escalation in the presentation rate. Upon the author's arrival there was an abundance of evidence that there had been more than a little prior "presentation." Upon the basis of the evidence gathered as a participant observer, the author concluded that such "presentation" is a fixed and all but indispensable feature of the deliberations of this august body.

The primary term of public service which renders it an all but insupportable burden in many cases is the requirement that all members of the Authority remain in the high pueblo throughout their term of office. An intense, extremely particularized transhumance is the *sine qua non* of Yoleño subsistence. Yolox is a ceremonial center and the villagers live all over the municipio. They congregate in the pueblo or disperse among the dependent hamlets in response to the centripetal imperatives of the political and religio-ceremonial cycles and the centrifugal requirements of the agricultural cycle. The question "Do most of the people live in the pueblo or in the hamlets?" always elicited surprise: "We are the same people, we all walk together. It is just that sometimes we live down there and sometimes we live up here!" (V. L. F. Field Notes.)

A year's permanent residence in the centrally located pueblo excludes the director of the family's subsistence activity from labor on plots in the area of the municipio, where most families derive the great bulk of their subsistence. Thus, for most families, the acceptance of public service obliges them to exist at an even more marginal level than is generally the case. Despite the many disadvantages associated with a call to public service it is hardly ever ignored. Even when civic virtue is its only reward, the majority of villagers prefer to bear these purely economic privations rather than incur the public opprobrium and secret malice of their paisanos.

The prerogatives and responsibilities of the Authority are set forth in the *Ley de Ayuntamiento* of the State of Oaxaca. This document is in turn in conformity with the Constitution of the United States of Mexico. The village Authority is, then, the mediator of the larger Republican tradition and the authoritative agent of the smaller, local Chinantec tradition. The Ayuntamiento, or Authority, is the instrument through which such national programs as the National Campaign against Onchocerciasis, the anti-malaria campaign, and the campaign for the eradication of illiteracy are interpreted and implemented on a municipal level.

Familiarity with the larger Republican tradition is one of the most eminent qualifications for responsible office in the village.

You see, those of my paisanos *who know something of these things of the Republic or the state, these learned ones are always the ones that are chosen for important charges. Now those of our poor* paisanos *who have had little time in school or who have not gone outside, they are the ones who have to be policemen. They must rise early at the bidding of the Authority and go with the sleep still in their eyes to Ixtlán or wherever the Authority wishes to send them.*

[P. L. F. FIELD NOTES]

All the proceedings of the Authority and the municipal archives are written in the language of the dominant state. Except for the use of Chinantec place names where extreme accuracy is a requirement, as in wills and formal land transactions, Chinantec, or *idioma,* as it is known locally, has no official place in the records of this organ of local government.

The offices of municipal president and *alcalde,* or justice, are the most prestigious positions in the Authority but the secretaries of these ranking executive and judicial members of the village Authority hold unique positions. They couch the requests and replies, queries and responses in the sonorous, respectful, written rhetoric characteristic of communications between San Pedro Yolox and Oaxaca de Juárez or Mexico City. In a corner of the world where something of the aura of innovation still clings to that prosaic diagnostic trait of the industrial inventory, the typewriter, a relative familiarity with that machine inspires a kind of respect which verges on awe.

The only member of the Authority who could not be said to have been a native son of the pueblo was the municipal secretary. Secretaries are generally better grounded in the civic and legal traditions of the larger Mexican society and assist in interpreting their finer points to the municipal executive and judicial officers. Reliance upon Zapotecans for the expedition of municipal affairs noted by some investigators in the area (Bevan 1938:28; de la Fuente 1949:115), however, does not appear to be the general rule in Yolox.

In addition to the municipal or presidential secretary, there is also a secretary to the alcalde, who advises that second-ranking officer on the general provisions of the *Ley Judicial* of the State of Oaxaca and handles his correspondence and written rulings. Three fiscal officers, or *regidores;* a *síndico,* or high constable; two police lieutenants, each commanding a squad of four *topiles,* or constables; and two *tecticlatls,* or porters, complete the personnel of the Authority.

The Authority has not yet been reduced to a mere appendage of Oaxacan and larger Mexican administration. Of course it functions in conformity with those wider systems but still preserves a strong local character. The Authority is a vigorous institution which commands great deference and its officers, speaking in its name, are persons of consequence. Nothing approximating that venality and corruption noted in other parts of rural Mexico

(Foster 1942:73; Lewis 1963:221–22) was discernible in the activities of the municipal Authority of San Pedro Yolox.

Accounts of notable incidences of arbitration or adjudication find their way into oral tradition. Fathers are especially inclined to recount these precedence tales to their sons for didactic purposes. These stories deal at length with the hard fate of pícaros brought before the Authority for some infraction. There is eyewitness evidence of the guilt of the offender in most stories and his punishment is taken for granted. In these stories it is not the gravity of the particular abuse of the public peace which augments the poor antihero's trials but his willfulness and defiance of the Authority of his pueblo. This defiance never is said to take the form of outright rudeness or impassioned statements of the rights of the accused, but is confined to a simple refusal on the part of the malefactor to admit that he knows the cause of his arrest or to plead. Each refusal to incriminate himself is the occasion of increasingly grave threats of dire castigation. This contest ends with the síndico or alcalde assuming an attitude of cold, austere, ironic anger, and commanding the lieutenant of police to order one of his topiles to bring a spade or some other gravedigging tool. The stern admonition of the presiding officer that another negative reply to the question "Why are you in this jail?" will set in motion the irreversible preparation for his incarceration in "that prison from which there is no escape" causes the pícaro to break and fling himself deferentially upon the mercy of the Authority.

New members of the Authority are chosen at a *junta* (public assembly) of all the male heads of families, who pay *cooperación,* or assessment, for the village fiestas. On the first day of the new year, at another junta, the old members pass on their ceremonial rods of office to the new personnel of the Authority during the solemn ceremony known variously as *El Año Nuevo* or *Flores de Pascua.*

On the second day of the new year there is a general junta at which a *Plan de Trabajo,* list of village projects, is formulated. On the third day of the new year at a third general junta of all the married male heads of families the new president receives custody of the village archives which are kept in the house of the chief executive. During the period of my stay the Plan de Trabajo called for the undertaking of such public works as the construction of a new school, the extension of the Ramal de Yolox down

New members of the Authority are chosen at a junta.

the flanks of Cerro Pelón to the village itself and the rebuilding of two bridges. The second broad general division of the pueblo work plan was devoted to village education and called for the institution of a plan to provide a meal a day for schoolchildren and the acquisition of school supplies. The third major division of this list of village projects was devoted to aspects of public health and called for the maintenance of the recently constructed Health Center and the cleaning of the village streets.

Juntas are called to debate or implement these and numerous other decisions respecting village welfare. The president can call one of these public assemblies whenever he deems it necessary. All male heads of families are obliged to attend upon pain of a fine of 6 pesos or a day in the one-celled village jail.*

The illness of a *contribuyente* or a member of his family is the only generally accepted excuse for his absence from a junta. In any case, the formal permission of the president must be obtained if a man cannot attend.

The Authority levies a tax of days of labor upon all able-bodied mature males called *tequio*. A man can either "do his tequio" by donating a varying number of actual days of labor for public works or pay in cash a specified

---

* In addition to the jail the public stocks in Rancho Esperanza can be used to confine as many as five prisoners in this centrally located hamlet until they can be taken to the high pueblo for formal legal action. The families of persons thus detained are responsible for feeding them. Crime does not, in this small primary community, pose a serious problem. The principal cause of public disorder is alcohol-inspired assault during fiestas which are invariably the occasions for even heavier drinking. The festival of San Isidro, one of the low-lying hot humid hamlets, which falls on May fifteenth, is traditionally reckoned to be especially likely to degenerate into an occasion when "men made *bravo* (bold) by too much strong drink will strike the people or grab a woman."

sum for each day of labor assigned him. The number of persons able to avail themselves of this latter provision is very small. The vast majority of men are obliged to do their tequio by the contribution of actual labor.

The number of days of tequio varies with the requirement for public service. If the rains are average or there is no ambitious public works project to be undertaken, then the assessment is light; but if many of the bridges are washed out and the cemetery is in grievous need of repair or some project like the construction of the new health center or a new school is embarked upon, then there must be attendant increase in the levy upon the time and muscle of every able son of the pueblo. The only provision for the waiving of this requirement is grave illness. In this instance also the Authority in the person of the president must approve all exemptions.

The village Authority still serves as a prestigious, final arbiter between spouses in serious discord, among families in grave public controversy and as a prime instrument of public order. With the single exception of the general prohibition of the participation of women of whatever degree of sagacity in its deliberations, the Authority is a fairly democratic assembly. One of its former chief executives is the wealthiest man in the village. Another former president lives in one of the poorest jacales and is economically one of the most disadvantaged men in the pueblo.

Much of the seeming arbitrariness in the functioning of the Authority and the respect bordering on dread which it enjoys are instrumental in the successful discharge of its heavy responsibilities. For it is the only village-wide regulatory agency among the personnel of 130 household subsistence teams in an environment of desperate marginality.

Villagers belong to 6 barrios, which are invariably mentioned in this order: Dolores, Rosario, San José, La Soledad, Santa Rosa, and San Nicolás. During the time of the forced removal and resettlement of dispersed Chinantec groups from the old site of San Pedro Yoloxeniquila, and for some time thereafter, Yoleño barrios were probably territorial units.

The question "Which barrio are we in now?"—frequently asked during walks about the village—often led to protracted consultation and various responses. The most prominent member of the barrio of San José rarely visits the high pueblo and so cannot be said to have any territorial association with it. Residence in a strictly defined geographical area is plainly not a prerequisite for membership in any given barrio association. New members are formally presented to the barrio associations of their fathers, but except for the rare incidence of a person wishing to change his traditional barrio allegiance, a new member's acceptance is automatic. Barrios make approximately the same demands upon their members that the pueblo as a whole does. The two *mayordomos* who direct the affairs of the barrio are chosen by the men of their barrio association. The election is generally unsought, or at least there is rarely any active solicitation of these posts. Indeed, the positions are often regarded as a somewhat less onerous burden than the wider public service.

The mayordomos of the 6 barrios are also responsible before the Authority for the levying of a special assessment, generally 2 pesos, for each contribuyente who is a member of their respective barrio associations.

The sacristans act as mayordomos for *el Socio de los Solteros*, the Society of the Unmarried. This group is responsible for one of the principal village-wide fiestas— that of the Virgin of the Holy Assumption which falls on August fifteenth. The Society of the Unmarried is a village-wide, interbarrio association which might better be called the Single Men's Society. Youths of from fifteen years of age join it and remain members until they marry. Married men may volunteer or be asked to contribute toward the cost of the society's fiesta. The unmarried are referred to as a collectivity but there are actually two associations, a vigorous institution for males and a weakly developed society for unmarried girls.

Barrio associations possess capital funds from which sons of the barrio may, with general consent of all the members, borrow. This source is increasingly neglected as members wishing to borrow are reluctant to air their cases before an open junta of all members of the association. It is the duty of the mayordomos of a barrio to call members to juntas. Paralleling the pueblo-wide Plan de Trabajo, there is a plan of projects which each barrio formulates under each successive mayordomía, generally to raise funds for their *cooperación*, or contribution, toward the village fiestas and to defray the cost of the celebration of the fiesta of the barrio. These projects may vary from the acquisition and rental of draft animals to the actual purchase of agricultural plots. A portion of the rent derived and a percentage of the cash accruing from the sale of a specified portion of the yield of barrio parcels is allocated as cooperación toward the most important village fiestas. A portion of revenue thus realized goes toward the expenses of the less important barrio fiestas and a percentage goes to the ongoing barrio fund.

Three of the 6 barrios, Dolores, Santa Rosa, and La Soledad, own small plots which are worked only by barrio members. The maize crops yielded by these plots are stored and sold to members of the respective barrio associations at a price considerably below the general price in the village stores. In the autumn when corn is relatively plentiful, or at least as plentiful as it ever becomes, it was sold for 3.5 pesos per kilo, while members of landholding barrio associations could obtain the same amount for 2 pesos.

There is a general sentiment of barrio solidarity which receives somewhat exaggerated public expression. Members of a barrio association are supposed to buy from one another and assist each other with the association and in their general dealings. The dominance of particularly familial self-interest and the marginality of most families, however, strongly limit the actual degree of real material mutual assistance among the members of any given group outside the individual's particular biological and ritual kin.

A prime item on the village inventory of self-criticism is the general assertion that "we do not wish to cooperate." Or, as a friend and informant, ascending the ladders of pueblo-wide and barrio service, puts it:

We say to someone, "Look here, señor, you have this duty or that responsibility and then most of us make it very hard for him to do this thing we called him to do. I do not mean to say that we are a pueblo of disobedient pícaros! No, most people here listen to their parents. It's just that people have a mouth to talk with so they talk. Sometimes people will say no or make someone wait or say a bad thing about someone they have just got finished calling to get something done that everyone wanted to get done. Sometimes people will do such a thing just because they can do it! My paisanos are not fools and we know very well what would happen if we behaved that way all the time—people just like to make a man sweat a little sometimes, even if it makes things bad for themselves. If a man feels like saying no to his own children when he could just as well say yes, what kind of a fool would expect the same man to say yes and deal correctly with him just because he should!"

[P. L. F. FIELD NOTES]

Some attribute this failing to the general isolation of the municipio. Others ascribe it to a "natural" tendency to subordinate all sets of obligation to those of the most immediate self-interest.

The mayordomía system is also the vehicle of the arrangement of village-wide fiestas. Upon the expiration of each village-wide fiesta, the president calls a junta to choose the mayordomo who will be charged with the management of that ceremony in the succeeding year.

Here our first fiesta *is the fifteenth of January,* Fiesta de Discípula (*Disciple*), *and everyone comes for that. And after the fifteenth of January comes Holy Week. And then after the* Fiesta *of Holy Week we celebrate the* Fiesta *of St. Peter, who is the patron of this* municipio. *After the* fiesta *of the patron we have the* Fiesta *of the Virgin of Ocotlán, which is the* fiesta *of the unmarried, which falls on August fifteenth. Then we have the* Fiesta Patria, *the day of National Independence, which we celebrate on the sixteenth of September. The* Fiesta *of All Souls lasts two days. Next we celebrate Christmas and then the fifteenth comes again.* [V. L. F. FIELD NOTES]

The fifteenth of January, the day of the Patron, the celebration of Independence and the All Souls' celebration are each administered by four mayordomos and represent the most prestigious summit of the ceremonial pyramid. Most fiestas are managed by only two mayordomos, a president and a secretary-treasurer. Each of the 6 barrio associations holds its own fiesta. Each of the 7 hot humid hamlets and the hot dry hamlet of Carrizal observe their respective festive days. Each family has an intricate schedule of reciprocal attendance at the village-wide, barrio association, and hamlet fiesta cycles of other pueblos in the vicinity of Yolox. Village ayuntamientos, barrio associations, school committees, and religious fraternal organizations of amicable communities in reasonable proximity officially invite their neighboring counterparts to share their fiestas.

All of the recurrent fiestas of the regularized cycles are indissoluble amalgams of both the sacred and the secular. Mass, mescal, music and fireworks are indispensable elements of all village-wide celebrations and most smaller observances. Such festive occasions range from a simple gathering in one of the three small wooden chapels in the hamlets to recite the rosary to the spectacular observances of the fiesta of the fifteenth of January which features such notable events as a giant fireworks display and the riding of recently corralled bulls by the young men of the pueblo.

Whatever their feelings about the distinction, most villagers accept a position in the mayordomía system when they are summoned. The mayordomo's primary responsibilities are fiscal and festive. He keeps a list of that number of the sons of the pueblo who are also sons of his barrio. He must see that a copy of this roster is presented to the Authority as the village Ayuntamiento assesses each barrio association according to the number of sons of the pueblo that association claims as members. He keeps the books of the association, duly notes the names of those who are in arrears in their contribution of days of labor to barrio projects, and supervises the preparation of barrio fiestas. The mayordomo has generally reluctantly accepted the mandate of his fellows to perform the thankless job of persuading each member of the collectivity, which has just chosen him, to distinguish themselves by placing the demands of their barrio association at least on a par with the requirements of their particular subsistence.

My parents said I should get married. I said I want to learn
more. How can we arrange it? What can we do? We know
you want to but we have no money. . . . So I was married
and now I have five children and I will maintain them so long
as I can. So then, if I remain strong and well, my children
and I will not die.   [R. J. FIELD NOTES]

Yolox is a pueblo of 207 nuclear families housed in 130
dwellings. These households are made up of a number of
related nuclear families comprising anywhere from 2 to
19 inhabitants. (See Tables 3 and 4.)

Most of these joint households have two dwellings.
There is a house in the ceremonial pueblo. This is generally the more substantial and carefully constructed
dwelling. There is generally a second, less pretentious
lowland dwelling situated on the downslope agricultural
plots. Of the total population of 973 persons all save 136
have residences both in the High Village and in the agricultural hamlets.

The family is the basic political, social and economic
unit in Chinantec society. Marriage is regarded as a

Table 3: *Distribution of inhabitants per household**

NUMBER OF HOUSEHOLDS	INHABITANTS PER HOUSEHOLD	
10	2	15.53% of total population
14	3	live in households of 2–4
17	4	members
11	5	
20	6	62.84% of total population
20	7	live in households of 5–10
10	8	members
9	9	
5	10	
3	11	
5	12	21.62% of total population
3	13	live in households of 11–19
1	14	members
1	16	
1	19	
130	837	

* Census data from the 1963 Village Census, *Archivo general de San Pedro Yolox.*

prime prerequisite to adult responsibility. Married males gather in relatively democratic assemblies or juntas to discuss and often resolve issues of moment before the pueblo. Each family is assessed according to its size and capacity to pay for a contribution toward the fund which finances the several fiestas which are the indispensable elements of social and ceremonial life.

Almost all families are relatively self-contained economic units which are directly responsible for their own subsistence. Most husbands are subsistence farmers, di-

Table 4: *Distribution of inhabitants per family**

TYPE OF DWELLING	NUMBER OF DWELLINGS	PERCENT OF TOTAL 130 DWELLINGS	NUMBER OF INHABITANTS	PERCENT OF TOTAL 837 INHABITANTS	NUMBER OF FAMILIES	PERCENT OF TOTAL 207 FAMILIES	AVERAGE NUMBER INHABITANTS PER FAMILY	AVERAGE NUMBER INHABITANTS PER HOUSEHOLD
1 Family	74	56.92	342	40.86	74	35.75	4.6	4.6
2 Family	39	30.00	307	36.67	78	37.68	3.9	7.9
3 Family	13	10.00	126	15.06	39	18.84	3.2	9.7
4 Family	4	3.08	62	7.41	16	7.73	3.9	15.5
TOTAL	130	100.00	837	100.00	207	100.00	3.6	6.4

* Data taken from 1963 Village Inhabitant Census, *Archivo general de San Pedro Yolox*.

recting the participation of other members of the family in this vital activity. Of the 130 heads of households listed on the 1963 Village Census* probably not more than a dozen consistently derive any appreciable portion of their income from nonagricultural pursuits.

There is a rough division of labor based primarily upon sex. In general, women organize the tasks necessary to the functioning of the household while field labor and its attendant tasks are the responsibilities of men. Although field labor is ideally man's work the absence or shortage of male laborers in the family often forces women into the fields. Children are introduced to skills and work habits which they must acquire to fulfill their respective roles in Yoleño society by a kind of familial apprenticeship. The precise age at which the serious training of boys and girls for their respective adult work roles begins varies considerably from family to family. Responses to questions about the integration of children in family economy ranged from "the children do nothing but cry for bread day after day" and "the children do nothing to help" to an extensive list of tasks vital to household economy performed by children. The most general practice, however, was summarized in the following manner:

Usually the girls begin at ten with housework. Boys begin to go to the field at seven or eight. At sixteen or seventeen, after eight years, they can do the work of a man. We teach them more softly than our fathers taught us. [P. E. FIELD NOTES]

The Yoleño family orders the work regime vital to its functioning as a cooperative economic unit with a division

* Data taken from the 1963 Village Head of Household Census, *Archivo general de San Pedro Yolox.*

of labor by sex. Men prepare certain ceremonial dishes especially those made from wild game. Women also perform field tasks especially the sowing of maize. Generally adults of both sexes are extremely reluctant to acknowledge any real competence in the tasks ascribed to persons of the opposite sex. Specialization does lead to a genuine lack of true proficiency in the skills of the opposite sex but this incapacity is often more apparent than real as the Chinantec of Yolox ascribe a rather high value to such incapacity. It is believed by both sexes that men experience much greater difficulty in performing female tasks than do women in the performance of male tasks. This is why the fate of the widow, lamentable though it is, is regarded as somewhat less hard than that of the widower. Many persons singled out one C. H., charged with the maintenance of himself and a young daughter, as an example of the pitiable plight of the lone adult male obliged "even to wash his own clothes." Such is the desire to contract a second marriage that a recently widowed man walked to the village from the agencia of Temextitlán to secure my assistance in obtaining a bride. His journey was made all the more arduous by a serious foot deformity. It was only after advice had been vainly sought relative to romance that he inquired about means of correcting the aforementioned physical defect.

The contribution of years of useful labor to a family validates the claim of elderly or disabled members for support. This attitude was summed up in the following manner by an elderly blind informant:

Now I don't do anything, I am led by the hand, but I was a campesino *for more than sixty years. I worked in Rancho*

*Bobo and Esperanza too. So I earned my rest when I was
sound, as everyone does.*   [B. H. Q. FIELD NOTES]

The existence of a number of elderly blind persons imposes a heavy additional burden directly upon 21 households of the village. This set of obligations impinges
somewhat less onerously upon those linked by ties of
fictive consanguinity. An examination of 48 households
containing 80 nuclear families reveals that a minimum of
347 Yoleños (41.46 percent of the total High Village
population) are related in some way to the 21 blind inhabitants of Yolox. An examination of all the High Village households would doubtless reveal an even greater
number of persons directly or indirectly related to the
Yoleño blind (see Table 5).

There is all but universal agreement among Yoleños
that an individual's first allegiance is to his family. More-
over, most persons say that their own personal interests
ought to be subordinated to those of the family. There is
an attendant obligation on the part of an individual's
family to support him in disputes with members of other
families. This latter obligation is, however, hedged about
with so many qualifications that it is often rendered
almost inoperative. If it can be demonstrated that the
family member displayed overt anger in his or her dispute
with a member of another family his immediate kin may
refuse to second him. Such disputes may be submitted by
the head of one of the antagonistic families to the Roman
Catholic priest for reconciliation or, occasionally, adjudication. The counsel of the priest affords both parties to
the disagreement an opportunity to retire from their positions of public animosity as it is proverbial in Yolox that

Table 5: *Relationship to blind among inhabitants of forty-eight selected households**

TYPE OF RELATIONSHIP	NUMBER OF FAMILIES	PERCENT OF SELECTED FAMILIES	NUMBER OF HOUSEHOLDS	PERCENT OF SELECTED HOUSEHOLDS	NUMBER OF INHABITANTS	PERCENT OF SELECTED INHABITANTS	MINIMUM PERCENT OF TOTAL HIGH VILLAGE INHABITANTS RELATED TO BLIND
Kinship only	30	37.50	21	43.75	140	40.35	16.73
Marriage only	1	1.25	1	2.08	9	2.59	1.08
Compadrazgo only	9	11.25	5	10.42	38	10.95	4.54
Kinship and marriage	10	12.50	5	10.42	34	9.80	4.06
Kinship and compadrazgo	23	28.75	10	20.83	89	25.65	10.63
Marriage and compadrazgo	2	2.50	2	4.17	5	1.44	.60
Kinship, marriage, and compadrazgo	5	6.25	4	8.33	32	9.22	3.82
TOTAL	80**	100.00	48	100.00	347	100.00	41.46

* Representing 36.92 percent of total 130 village households.
** Representing 38.65 percent of total 207 families.

no man should be "bravo" before the priest. Senior members of both families may invoke their generational authority if the disputants are their juniors and persuade both antagonists to reassume public positions of amity.

Although people speak of feuding and threaten each other jocularly with this extremity there does not appear to be any institutionalized form of vendetta among Yoleño families. Feuding upon an intercommunal level, however, is the most important element of pueblo history as locally viewed. It may very well be that the fully efficient development of intercommunal feuding is instrumental in the weak development of intravillage vendetta.

Male dominance is the readily observable rule both in intrafamily interaction and in relations between families. The direction of the political affairs of the municipio is also "man's work." The conduct of the vital ceremonial round and the formal organization of its attendant fiestas are exclusively in male hands. The Single Men's Society is far more important and more widely supported than is the very rudimentary Single Women's Society. Husbands are ideally supposed to preside over all family funds. Male heads of families are the proper persons to make all momentous decisions about the frequent shifts in residence that almost all families are obliged to make during the year.

Yoleño men generally professed a belief in the genetic, mental inferiority of women as a group and were of the opinion that all their paisanos, women as well as men, shared this belief. It is further maintained that this disparity between the mental capacities of the sexes is of divine origin. This theory was first expounded to me by a blind man who was as close to being a patriarch as his particular disability and the peculiar circumstances of village life would permit. The Chinantec are generally a soft-spoken people but I noted a perceptible increase in this tendency toward the *sotto voce* almost invariably accompanied any exposition of the above-mentioned theory. Such opinions were never volunteered in the presence of women.

This belief in the "natural" inability of women to measure up to masculine standards of rationality sometimes functions to prevent the disruptive consequences of prolonged strife between spouses. If the dispute is not of grave nature and more especially if there is reason to think that it has not become public knowledge, males may acquiesce with a show of magnanimous condescension, dismissing the whole matter as mere feminine folly.

The double standard is a basic element in the culture of the village. Women are thought to be under much stronger obligation to do those things which the culture deems morally imperative and to refrain from doing those things which it prohibits. The burden of maintaining moral standards which, though applicable to all, are especially binding upon women, falls heaviest upon all pubescent females. In a community where alcoholism is a major problem,* the only person singled out for protracted

---

* In addition to the many interviews which were postponed or terminated prematurely because of the intoxication of the subject, at least 20 men are unable to work for periods of ten days as a result of nonfiesta drinking. Every day of my stay in the village I encountered at least one inebriated person. In addition to the brisk business done in *chingare* (raw crude cane alcohol) and sweet red wine in all the stores of the High Village, three men sell chingare, beer, and wine in Ranchos Chirrimoya and Esperanza. Mescal and chingare are sold in Ranchos San Juan and San Francisco and in the municipal agencias of San Martín Buena Vista and Temextitlán.

A man might very well spend as much as 60 pesos in a fiesta's drinking for himself and his friends. There is very little solo drink-

criticism was a woman who, within the privacy of her own home, was said to drink to excess: "It is a very ugly thing for her to do. If she were a man it would be a little less shameful" (R. J. Field Notes).

Extramarital sexuality is not severely condemned in males, whereas females thought to be guilty of such behavior are singled out for opprobrium and ridicule.

In a culture which discourages direct, publicly expressed antipathies gossip is very likely to be one of the most formidable means of indirect covert aggression at the disposal of aggrieved parties. Gossip is commonly supposed to be the particular province of lazy housewives. But the most cursory observation reveals that many individuals of both sexes and all degrees of diligence are often heavily engaged in the surreptitious increase and diffusion of malicious hearsay.

The "good" family is not one which is able to refute malicious rumors but one which is not mentioned excessively. The clandestine character of gossip makes it practically impossible to challenge it without that kind of open confrontation which the whole society would denounce as cowardice. The only culturally approved alternative open to the person thus injured is to set in motion his or her own campaign of clandestine slander. Thus the prime defense against gossip is the prime factor in its escalation. Gossip is a strong deterrent to change. It

ing, rather it is done with one's lifelong friends. Then the normal reserve which characterizes interpersonal relationships is swept away and fights frequently occur. Both the municipal president and the alcalde were in accord in citing assault occasioned by intoxication as the single most serious cause of crime in the municipio. At least 3 High Village families allot precious garden space to the cultivation of *yerba de borracho* (the herb of drunkenness), a local plant said to possess curative powers for the aftereffects of intoxication.

reinforces the tendency of most families to act as self-contained units which respond with apprehension and excessive suspicion to more broadly based economic or social projects. A case in point is that of the young village woman who had completed primary school and was briefly employed as a teacher. She soon became the target of such a sustained campaign of gossip that her father obliged her to withdraw from the school. He made no secret of his reasons for removing her and even the most inveterate gossipmongers admitted that the purveyors of rumor had gone too far. The Zapotecan schoolmasters are not fluent in Chinantec while the maligned teacher was a native Chinantec-speaker. But within a day of her removal surreptitious speculation was rife as to the persons most responsible for the excess in rumor, the "real" reasons why old José had withdrawn the girl and the appearance of the child which reliable persons were certain she was going to bear.

Families strive to keep themselves to themselves. Ideally women are not supposed to travel unaccompanied. Married women are hardly ever encountered away from their homes alone. They are most frequently accompanied by a child.

Male dominance is an important element in the culture of the Chinantec of Yolox. However, it functions as a general rule rather than an iron law. As a rule it could not objectively be called flexible but it is not so rigid that it ignores those circumstances which alter cases. Eleven of the 130 persons listed as heads of households on the village roster are women (8.46 percent).*

* Data taken from 1963 Village Head of Household Census, *Archivo general de San Pedro Yolox.*

The rigorous, complex agricultural regime and its consequent specialization along sexual lines forces a kind of mutual accommodation. Women's work is vital to the functioning of the family as an economic unit. The culture places a high value on feminine submissiveness but certain *pro forma* action patterns make this acquiescence appear even more general and profoundly imbedded than it is. Women say that they act out the submissive part but in many cases "the women keep the household going."

Patrilocality is the ideal and most common form of residence. Although some daughters bring husbands home marriage often entails for girls a separation from their most natural partisans (see Table 6).

Early marriage is frequent. Somewhat more than one-third of the women in the age group fourteen to nineteen are already married, according to official Mexican census figures. And two-thirds of all males in the age group twenty to twenty-four are listed as married (VIII censo general de población 1963 [I] :631). The first months or even years a bride spends in the household of her husband are looked upon as a kind of tutelary period in which

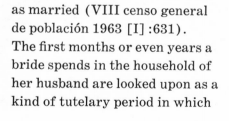

Women say they "keep the household going."

her mother-in-law is especially responsible for perfecting her in woman's work. The rigor of this period of adjustment and subordination varies with the personality set of her mother-in-law. If the senior woman's personality inclines toward austerity or if her own marital existence has been especially hard or degrading she may make the integration of the new member into full family membership a prolonged and painful process. It is said that a drunkard makes his wife a "bitter" mother-in-law. If, however, the elder woman is of a sanguine disposition and her own marriage has been subject to no more than those stresses which are regarded as "natural," i.e., poverty, illness, premature death of children,* etc., the new bride may be welcomed as a daughter and initiated with relative gentleness into full family status.

Husbands frequently compare this initial training of their brides to the breaking of an animal to draft labor. In describing this period of initial adjustment, male informants employ such phrases as "she knew nothing at first, when she first came to us she had to be taught everything" and "she was like a mule when she first came to us."

Yoleño marriages are arranged. Romantic love, though not unknown, is not an operative factor in the choice of a prospective mate. Yolox is a small primary community. The villagers evaluate each other upon the basis of intimate face-to-face contact. It is every father's responsibil-

---

* Eighty-five percent of families interviewed report at least one dead minor child. Of the 340 births recorded in the official village Birth Registry during the years 1958 to 1963, only 140 children five years old and under still appear on the village Inhabitant Census of 1963. As the population of the village is not greatly affected by out migration, death is undoubtedly the prime factor in the disparity.

ity to secure a good wife for his son. A father is also duty-bound to transfer his custody of his daughter to a good husband. Every eligible girl in the pueblo has been evaluated as to her obedience and industriousness. Any one of those with the best reputations for these highly prized qualities will be regarded as a good choice for a mate. The young men of the village are similarly ranked with more emphasis upon their capacity for hard work than upon docility and any one of them who is not regarded as being extraordinarily lazy or quarrelsome is deemed a suitable spouse.

Marriage is a prerequisite to the attainment of adult status so almost all potential mates are eligible. Indeed, the only persons in the village for whom all but insurmountable difficulty was predicted in finding a marriage partner were a youth of eighteen who had been injured in the fighting with the neighboring pueblo of Comaltepec and a blind girl of fifteen.

Marriages are "arranged" but the actual working of the social process is somewhat less arbitrary than that term implies. The arrangement is the sole responsibility of the fathers of the prospective couple only in those cases which closely approximate the cultural ideal. Parents frequently oblige their sons to give up a bachelor existence, especially if the family is subject to grave economic stress. The young man may be free to choose among the eligible young women of the municipio to whom he is especially attracted and with whom he has especially cordial relationships.

Extreme constraint is either ruled out or mitigated considerably by the extrafamilial aspect of the social process. The arranging of a marriage not only involves the social participation of the immediate biological kin of the potential spouses but sets in motion the formidable machinery of fictive consanguinity. The godparents of marriage assume that role which Yoleño distaste for direct social intercourse has elevated above all other prestigious roles. The amicable intermediaries represent the interests of the persons most directly concerned. Godparents of marriage are acquainted with the practical considerations which are likely to motivate both sets of parents and are familiar with and, more likely than not, sympathetic to the feelings of their respective fictive children.

The Ayuntamiento, or municipal Authority, is traditionally ascribed the role of final arbiter in cases of extreme arbitrariness on the part of parents. It cannot interpose its will unless invited to do so by any one of the parties to the case. But once any interested party has requested the intercession of the Authority all members are under a solemn injunction to present the matter for adjudication. If the Ayuntamiento finds that undue coercion has been brought to bear it may order the party or parties which it deems principally at fault to be jailed for a day and a night and impose a fine of as much as 60 pesos. Needless to say, the incidences of such appeals to the ultimate authority are extremely rare. Concurrent with the general reluctance to "carry things to Mexico," that is, to invoke the juridical machinery of the Mexican Republic, there is a reluctance to appeal to the highest local authority.

The actual scene of arrangement is the house of the godparents of matrimony. The ceremony of the *mitad* (the half), also conducted at the house of the groom's godparents of matrimony, symbolizes the successful end of negotiations and the cultural recognition of the legal status of the new family. In the ceremony of the mitad the prospective groom offers half of any sweet to the prospective bride. A cup of well-sweetened coffee or chocolate, *panela* (loaf sugar), honey or candy purchased in the stores may be shared. The sweet is offered in the presence of both sets of parents and godparents. If the young woman accepts and consumes the sweet she has committed herself to sharing half of the groom's lot in life.

The ceremony of the mitad marks the conclusion of a series of extremely civil, guarded exchanges. The young man's godparents of matrimony are under an obligation to facilitate the general atmosphere of cordiality by providing cigarettes and mescal when negotiations have reached an advanced state. Nowadays, beer or even wine, both prestige beverages, may be substituted for mescal. These negotiations end formally with the godfather of matrimony of the groom asking the father of the bride if he consents to the union.

A wedding feast and dance are held in the house of the groom. The cost of these wedding fiestas and the household goods which the new couple will need to establish a family are borne by the family of the groom. The purchasing of turkeys for the preparation of the traditional prestige food for weddings, turkey *mole,* the hiring of musicians and the acquisition of the blankets, sleeping mats, yard goods, pots, metates, and other household goods often obliges the family of the groom to incur a formidable burden of indebtedness at the stores. Families are very often obliged to pledge stock or parcels of land as security. Loans of cash to defray the cost of a wedding may be granted by the Barrio Association. The same kind of security is demanded. Actual instances of recourse to this means of financing appear to be rare. Generally, people prefer to go directly to one of the three larger stores of the High Village. There they choose the goods, ascertain their value, pledge security and arrange for payment.

The foregoing description is of the preferred form of marriage. Most informants stressed the dedication of the municipio to the Roman Catholic faith. Church marriage is the rule,* but other forms of socially accepted unions exist. Civil marriage appears to be the rarest form. In most of the cases of civil marriage reported there were subsequent ecclesiastical ceremonies. Civil marriage is not thought of as complete without the fully validating church rite. Informants were anxious to register their opinion that church marriage is the only binding form. Informants expressed open anxiety about the recording of their own marriage form. Often repeated assurances that the reply was understood were necessary during the course of an interview.

One of the most ardent detractors of any but the clerical ceremony was himself a party to that kind of socially recognized sexual alliance which holds an intermediate position between church marriage and civil marriage, namely, the consensual union. This man plainly preferred the clerical form to his own arrangement and thought I would esteem that form more highly. A sixty-eight-year-

---

* Republican census data indicate that of 855 married individuals in the entire municipio, 661 are parties to religious ceremonies only, 120 are parties to civil marriages with the "validating" church rite, 44 have contracted consensual unions, while 30 have contracted civil ceremonies only (VIII Censo general de población 1963[I]:631).

old blind informant, questioned concerning his marital status replied, "I have a woman, but I am not married. I never did marry. I have two sons though" (V. J. Field Notes).

First marriages are more likely to be church marriages. Second unions are celebrated with a minimum of ceremony and are more likely to be consensual unions than first marriages. The primary factor in the development of the consensual union appears to be the need to restore the efficiency of the family as a minimal productive unit. The complementary roles of both men and women are vital to the proper functioning of the family as a relatively autonomous subsistence unit. The press of circumstance obliges most spouses constrained by the death or occasional desertion of a marriage partner to assume the work roles of both sexes. Persons thus disadvantaged strive to end what is regarded as a tolerable but "unnatural state of affairs" as soon as possible. The villagers speak of a year's waiting period between the death of a spouse and remarriage as being appropriate. But the surviving spouses generally wait only as long as they have to.

There are a number of women who are not parties to any of the three forms of socially approved unions who are mothers of one or more children. There are, according to the 1963 Village Census, 62 widows and 14 widowers in the High Village. Anyone wishing to consummate a second union knows how many other persons are desirous of forming one. The imperatives of subsistence generally and the peculiar circumstances of his own case guide his choice of one of the potential partners. While most people charged the woman from Quiotepec (a nearby village) who remarried within a month after the death of her husband with shameless haste the remarriage of a paisano within four months of the death of his wife was not greeted with any opprobrium.

Perhaps because they are based on essentially the same imperatives consensual unions appear to be as stable as any other pattern of sexual union. C. V. and P. A. formed a consensual union in the mid-twenties which is still viable. M. M., a blind man, has lived in consensual union with D. F. for twenty years. S. B. and R. O. formed a consensual union when they were both well into their sixties. In addition to the traditional matter-of-factness which the culture associates with a second sexual alliance many persons are reluctant to incur the costs of the more formal and elaborate arrangement. Many of the persons entering consensual unions are past the age where they might rely upon the aid of their families in defraying the cost of the most preferred form of marriage. Such persons are often burdened with the support of one or more minor children, a circumstance which may render the cost of an elaborate second ceremony entirely beyond their means. Children of such unions are officially registered as *"natural"* in contradistinction to *"legítimo,"* * but it is difficult to detect even the mildest social disapprobation of these children.

There is a device operative in the culture which functions to remove much of the onus of that social stigma

* The official Yoleño birth registry often reflects a kind of humorous informality which derives from the face-to-face relations which are characteristic of the municipio. The terms legitimate and natural are not employed with any great consistency and nicknames, humorous and even obscene asides frequently are found. The degree of official attention to detail or whimsy depends upon the diligence and temperament of the recorder.

which attaches to women who have given birth outside the culturally sanctioned forms of marriage, namely, fictive widowhood—that is, the ascription of a widow's status to any woman who has borne and is charged with the maintenance of minor children. It must be pointed out, however, that the ascription of widowhood is by no means an unalloyed act of social charity. The wider application of the term cannot be said to have enhanced it much. Indeed, the ascription has occasioned a rather acute abasement of the status.

The widow is the dominant character of Yoleño ribaldry. The word *widow,* in addition to its conventional connotation, is used interchangeably to mean: a sweetheart, a woman with a reputation for sexual promiscuity, any woman with an "abnormal" interest in sex. Local census data take no official notice of the wide variation in meaning and these distinctions are not readily apparent. They emerge with familiarity with the people. Persons of both sexes refer to fictive and actual widows in the same way in general conversation. Fictive widows are aware, of course, of the adverse aspects of their ascribed status but rare indeed is the occasion upon which they are directly embarrassed. Older women whose widowhood is not fictive are mildly annoyed at the deflation of their status occasioned by the ascription of it to their younger and less circumspect sisters. This pique occasionally creeps into their voices but they would not dream of giving the game away to strangers consciously. It cannot be emphasized too strongly that it is the status generally which has been devalued and not any given individual's personal standing. The Yoleño's particularizing about his paisano is every bit as rigorous as his generalizing about the people of neighboring pueblos.

The elderly woman who is actually a widow is sometimes annoyed at the cultural ascription of widowhood but her dissatisfaction does not go beyond annoyance because she knows that her paisanos are making the same distinctions among holders of this status as she is. The woman to whom widowhood has been socially ascribed is aware of the same distinctions. As one young man put it: "there are widows and widows and we know the difference" (C. F. Field Notes). The effect of ascribed widowhood upon village residence patterns is indicated in Table 6.

The formal reason most often cited for the social ascription of widowhood is the protection it is said to afford minor children, especially boys. The ascription of widowhood provides *pro forma* evidence of legitimate paternity and elevates the child from the deplorable status of *"bastardo"* to the highly ambivalent intermediate position of "orphan." Fictive widowhood does not satisfy fully the ego needs of the parties involved. It functions to avoid polarity. It accords all children of the pueblo a tolerable if not a particularly exalted public status and leaves the individual free to make whatever private, informal reservations he may choose. The expression of any such reservations, especially if they are negative or at variance with conventional opinions, is generally confined within the family, which strives to keep its own counsel.

The primary mitigating factor in the intense familistic particularity is the pervasive binding social mechanism of *compadrazgo* (ritual, fictive kinship). Families of differing wealth levels residing in diverse territorial subdivi-

Table 6: *Residence patterns of sixty-four* households containing married children and widowed** daughters*

FAMILY COMPOSITION	NUMBER OF HOUSEHOLDS	PERCENT OF HOUSEHOLDS CONTAINING MARRIED CHILDREN
Married sons only	37	57.82
Married sons and married daughters	8	12.50
Married sons and widowed** daughters	5	7.81
TOTAL PATRILOCAL HOUSEHOLDS	50	78.13
Married daughters only	6	9.38
Married sons and married daughters	8	12.50
Married and widowed** daughters	2	3.13
TOTAL MATRILOCAL HOUSEHOLDS	16	25.01
Widowed** daughters only	6	9.38
TOTAL ASCRIBED MATRILOCAL HOUSEHOLDS	6	9.38
TOTAL MATRILOCAL HOUSEHOLDS INCLUDING THOSE ASCRIBED	27	42.19

* Representing 49.23 percent of the total 130 households.
** Most are probably fictive widows who have remained in the household of their fathers.

sions of the village, municipio, and district are linked in stable alliances of ascribed, ritual consanguinity. The overwhelming majority of such alliances are between families with differing barrio associations. In a number of cases this net of ritual kinship extends beyond the district of Ixtlán, establishing ties of varying strength between village families and families in other parts of the state of Oaxaca and even beyond.

The compadrazgo tie is thought of as an injunction of the Catholic faith. Godparents are selected with extreme care. The dominant consideration in the choice is the welfare of the child. The highest categories of this relationship imply a heavy responsibility. These weighty obligations are held to be sacred. To accept the request to become a godparent is regarded as a meritorious act which will be rewarded in the "other world." To refuse an invitation to become a co-parent for any but the most compelling extenuating circumstances is to incur both divine censure and the most enduring enmity of one's paisanos.

The most important kinds of compadrazgo relationships are attendant upon the ritual recognition of the passage of the individual along the crisis continuum from birth to death. The most onerous of these acts of obligation are those incurred by godparents of baptism. Godparents of baptism are obliged to purchase the baptismal garments of their godchild. In the event of the death of the biological kin of their godchild, godparents of baptism are expected to rear the orphaned youngster as a member of their own family. The provision of grave clothing for a deceased godchild and mescal and cigarettes for the funeral observance is the responsibility of the godparents of baptism. There are some individuals who have acted as godparents of baptism and of matrimony for the same godchild. Informants indicate that this is general practice.

The next most serious compadrazgo tie is that incurred by those invited to become godparents of matrimony. The managing of the delicate interfamily diplomacy attendant upon matrimonial negotiations is their responsibility. They too must purchase the cigarettes and strong drink which facilitate conviviality at the fiesta which celebrates the successful conclusion of these negotiations. There are two more generally diffused and less grave kinds of compadrazgo relationships common in the village, those of confirmation and the candle.

Godparents of confirmation incur no mandatory financial burden. They are simply to accompany their godchild of confirmation to the church and remain there during the service as sponsors. Parties to this kind of compadrazgo relationship may present their godchild with a gift. Shoes or ready-made clothing are regarded as especially appropriate and prestigious and such generosity, while not obligatory, is said to indicate *mas cariño* (more love) for the godchild.

The most common compadrazgo tie is that known in some regions of the Sierra Juárez as the rosary (de la Fuente 1949:170) and in Yolox as the candle, or the altar. In this least formal relationship the godparents of the candle take the child to the church and light candles of varying size as propitiatory offerings. This rite is a response to some crisis, generally illness, in the life of a young child. If the rite is deemed efficacious the child is taken to church a second time and a "candle of thanks" is lit. This form of godparentage generally involves very little expense to the persons assuming it. Some families report that they themselves purchased the candles which their co-parents of the candle offered. As the prayers of the virtuous and the afflicted are thought to be especially efficacious persons known to have lived an exemplary life and the blind are especially sought out as co-parents of the candle. Some informants report as many as 150 such ties.

The gravity and respect of godparent-godchild relations and the reciprocal deferential behavior of co-parents increases with the seriousness of the particular kind of compadrazgo tie uniting them. The polite *Usted* form is correct for all compadrazgo relationships. A godchild should employ it in addressing his godfather of the candle and his godparents of baptism, confirmation or matrimony. In actual practice, however, the *Usted* deferential form of address is most scrupulously adhered to only in the kinds of ritual kin ties based on baptism and marriage.

The most formal and binding forms of campadrazgo are often characterized by a client-patron relationship. Along with the tendency to invite the long-suffering and the pious, irrespective of wealth, to become godparents of the candle and confirmation, there is a converse inclination to seek ritual kin alliances with wealthier families for baptism and marriage. All the persons regularly retained as herders, carriers, and general servants by the four wealthiest village households were linked to their employers by some degree of ritual kinship, most often one of the more serious ties. Companía agreements very often join co-parents of differing wealth levels in some cooperative venture.

The compadrazgo tie does not only link *ahijado* with *padrino* and *madrina*, godchild with godfather and godmother, and the biological parents of the godchild with the godparents as *compadres*, or co-parents, but unites all close kin of both families. Co-parents regard each other as being affinally linked and sexual relations among god-siblings or co-parents are regarded as incestuous. "It is as though we are brothers."

Parties to all co-parent relationships were named friends or best friends, but the more respectful the relationship, the lower was the correlation between it and intimate amity.

Quite apart from its high status as a religiously enjoined social institution and its vital economic role facilitating the exchange of time, labor, and deference for limited access to land, stock, or cash, compadrazgo functions as a kind of customary insurance. For the selection of godparents of the most serious grades is

a very delicate business. If a man does not wish to make an orphan of his child, he must go carefully. For who but a fool will swear that God will give him a long life. And if He does, will He not take the sight of his eyes or the strength of his arms first? Then how will it be for the children if they have no godparents?   [V. L. G. FIELD NOTES]

The only public part played by women in the religio-ceremonial life of the village is as ritual godmothers in two minor village fiestas. Some time immediately before Christmas an adult woman of the village holds a fiesta at her house which any villager may attend. The woman who sponsors and presides over this fiesta is called the godmother of the pueblo.

On the sixth of January a prepubescent girl called the godmother of the infant Jesus leads a solemn procession composed largely of women bearing the image of Christ to church. Both the godmother of the pueblo and the godmother of the infant Jesus are materially seconded in the preparation of their respective fiestas by their kin, biological and ritual.

Some measure of the vitality of the compadrazgo system may be deduced from the fact that villagers tend to remember deceased ritual kin more readily than dead biological relations when listing their relatives.

A prime factor in the persistence and vigor of ritual kinship among the villagers is its sheer usefulness as a validating device for claims for assistance. It is proverbial in Yolox that "it is the favor that begets friendship." While villagers "honor the faith by seeking co-parents" they are also perpetuating a social mechanism which facilitates practical interaction within and between families on a day-to-day basis. Each family's preoccupation with its own generally desperate subsistence effort is so intense that villagers discount mutual assistance across kin lines. That sense of the essential isolation of families and adult individuals described for other peasant communities (de la Fuente 1949:162–64; Foster 1962:50; Lewis 1963:58, 59) is pervasive in Yolox.

"Here it's every man with his own burden. My neighbors are deaf to the barking of my belly" (P. L. A. Field Notes).

My father and my grandfather told me about a man, one of my paisanos, *who was very bad. When he was clean and sound he was a sacristan, but he was always drunk. He could drink mescal by the jug and* chingare *and anything that would make him a fool! Now he took money from the church to buy all that strong drink. But then he started to have headaches and little pieces of trash began to fall from his eyes and then his eyes were closed completely. Everybody said that it was for his bad faith in his charge of sacristan that he was stricken.*

[P. L. F. FIELD NOTES]

The first evidence of the existence of onchocerciasis in Mexico dates from 1925 (Strong 1934:50) but *mal de la ceguera* (the blinding sickness)—the local designation for the acute degenerative later stages of onchocerciasis—is a firmly established negative expectation among Yoleños. Yoleño culture is synchronic, almost exclusively concerned with its own present. The price of a tape recorder or a typewriter is a matter of absorbing interest to almost everyone, but the origin and mechanics of such devices are not. A very small minority of villagers know that the ox, the orange, and the blinding sickness "came with the Spaniards," but most villagers simply are not given to diachronic conjecturing about the customary.

Both the blinding sickness and its gravest consequence —total or economic blindness—are elements of the customary.

Divine or human intervention is, in the traditional Chinantec view, an instrumental agency in most illness and misfortune. There are a number of methods of divination which are useful in discovering the source, cause and possible cure of some illnesses or misfortunes. V. G. ate three mushrooms the size of a woman's fist to discover "why it went so badly with her life." After inquiring of her why they had been eaten, the mushrooms summoned her grandmother. The old woman told her that her life was being made "unlucky" by the anger of her grandfather. V. G. had not shown the proper respect for the old man in his life and he was now rewarding her "disobedience" from his vantage point in the "other world." The grandfather refused to speak to her, but her grandmother assured her that if she were to purchase masses for the dead in his honor he would be appeased and leave her life "to be what it would be" without the addition of his retributive malice. V. G. appealed to a sister in less marginal circumstances to lend 30 pesos for the purchase of the propitiatory masses. V. G. must return the money but she has good terms, a lengthy time period and no interest was charged as the entire family stood to gain from the assuaging of the grandfather's anger.

During the last series of bloody clashes between Yolox and Comaltepec, two Yoleño constables were seized some distance from their pueblo and held for several days. After three days the wife of one of the constables, anxious to learn her husband's fate, determined to

do the divination that is done with white maize. She filled a jícara *(gourd vessel) with water and threw three grains of white maize into that* jícara. *She knew that if the maize should sink that he was yet alive. If it did not sink, then she would know that he was surely dead. The maize sank and did not rise and she left off crying and said he would come tomorrow or the day after tomorrow, and in three days he came home.*   [R. E. FIELD NOTES]

Against illness or adversity occasioned by human beings in this world or the next there may be some remedy, but against grievous strokes laid on by divine will there is generally none. The blinding sickness was never attributed to sorcery. Expressions like "God closed his eyes completely," "God clouded his eyes" and "God ended his sight," in common usage among the villagers, indicate a common tendency to ascribe blindness to supernatural intervention.

Even those who offered a more secular explanation of blindness and the blinding sickness were more often influenced by local folk pathology rather than modern greater Mexican medical concepts. Indigenous Yoleño concepts of pathology are a synthesis of Iberian and Amerindian beliefs.

People can talk to the dead if they eat mushrooms. If the blood is cold they can eat three mushrooms. If the blood is hot then they can eat ten little ones and then they may speak to the dead.   [P. L. M. FIELD NOTES]

Thus the Iberian belief in hot and cold foods and states

of the blood has become indissolubly linked with the indigenous practice of "becoming drunk with the drunkenness that comes of eating mushrooms."

There does not appear to be any culture-wide remedy in the Yoleño folk pharmacopoeia for the blinding sickness. D. V. O.'s wife chewed the leaves of the plant called *siempre viva* and spat the juice upon a cloth with which she washed his eyes three times a day. Siempre viva is thought to have general curative powers but its use in this particular instance for this particular purpose was suggested by a priest who was not a Chinantec.

Blindness is sometimes attributed to *susto*, or shock, caused by abrupt changes in body temperature.

If a man works in his fields down in the ranchos *where the air is hot and wet, he sweats very much. Then when he comes up to the pueblo where the air is fresh and cool he foolishly takes off his shirt and the change in air gives his body a shock* [susto] *and he becomes blind.* [M. P. FIELD NOTES]

The widespread habit of removing the shirt during arduous agricultural labor exposes a greater portion of the male body to bites of the intermediate hosts. This difference in the amount of exposed body surface may be a factor in the slightly higher infection rate for men (García Sánchez and Chávez Núñez 1962:954).

Both blind and sighted persons frequently advanced impiety as a cause of the blinding sickness. This "Pedro who, in cold sobriety, struck his father"—that "Patrocina that was a liar and a scold from her youth and who behaved so savagely to her own children"—that "Pablo who cared nothing for his holy charge, but stole God's money to make himself drunk and did all kinds of bad things which the people did not like in plain sight of everyone" —"*Tata Dios* (God the Father) closed their eyes forever." The element of arbitrariness is inextricably associated with most villagers' thinking about acts of God. It is axiomatic in Yolox that "God does as He pleases."

An informal registry of the onchocercous blind is kept in the municipal archives, largely for the records of the National Campaign against Onchocerciasis. Campaign samples list 85 totally blind persons in the Oaxaca endemic zone, 16 of whom live in Yolox. It is officially estimated that the number of economically blind persons is double that of the totally blind. Five totally blind persons then not formally registered with any official agency were interviewed during the course of this study. I discovered only two individuals in the blind population of the municipio who were non-onchocercous blind—a girl of fifteen, blind since birth and an adult male who lost one hand and his sight as a consequence of an accident which occurred while he was "fishing with dynamite." Except for registration and exemption from communal assessment, the community takes no further official interest in the blind.

"Everyone's blindness is a cross which he and his kin must carry alone" (H. P. Field Notes).

The absence of a clearly defined concept of chronicity in the disease concepts of the villagers makes it very difficult for many people to accept the necessity for ongoing treatment. The fact that this ongoing treatment involves minor surgery, a suspect innovation among the Chinantec of Yolox, militates against its acceptance. The addition of therapeutic shock to the already formidable roster of environmental trauma Yoleños are subject to imposes a burden greater than the sum of the effect of mere adverse symptoms.

Acceptance of the standard course of treatment involves the acceptance of pain and even temporary incapacity. This suffering is not occasioned by any of the stressful agents the Chinantec have been transgenerationally conditioned to bear stoically. The Chinantec are culturally conditioned to accept the gravest consequence of onchocerciasis, blindness. Knowledge of the origin and course of the disease is not a part of that culture's experience. The general absence of spectacular initial symptoms, the lengthy course of the disease, and the fact that the entire germ theory is a poor second in the Chinantec concept of disease means that most villagers are obliged to accept the efficacy of the standard prescribed course of treatment on faith. A faith which must rely for its justification

"Everyone's blindness is a cross which he must carry alone."

upon evidence of things as yet unseen by Chinantec tradition is understandably qualified. The Chinantec of Yolox
are profoundly skeptical regarding their own traditional
ritual practices. This strong sense of the problematic derives from a general conviction that divinity and its en-
gine, the forces of nature, are not necessarily bound by
any act of man.

The greater Mexican concept of the pathology of onchocerciasis is one item in the vast inventory of greater
Mexican traits and concepts which constitute the vacil-
lating unstructured tide of change.

Response to a particularly intensive program of diagnosis and treatment in a pilot zone (Aranda Villamayor
1963:51–69) which included Yolox varied from only 30
to 90 persons out of a 100. This variation in positive response was frankly ascribed to the degree of pressure
brought to bear by local authorities in the several communities of the pilot zone. The majority of the people of
the pilot zone which includes San Pedro Yolox, Santiago
Comaltepec, and a portion of San Juan Quiotepec resisted
diagnosis and treatment.

Recognizing the need to combine the medical effort with
a broadly based social and economic program, the National Campaign against Onchocerciasis linked treatment
with the general effort to introduce change through such
cultural catalytic institutions as the school and the Health
Center. The school treatment is said to be meeting with a
positive response which is reflected in diagnostic surveys.

An increasing minority of school-aged children in Yolox
do attend school, generally at great cost to their families.
Sports clubs appeal to young men even after formal connection with the school is terminated. Access to sewing

machines at the Health Center constructed jointly by communal and national effort is intended to attract village housewives to the Center and its program.

This broadly based effort to link diagnosis and treatment with general alteration of the extreme marginality common to Yolox and other onchocerciasis infected communities as yet does not engage the vast majority, especially the decision-making segment of these communities.

The principal role of this element in Yolox is as intermediate figures of suasion. The local Authority brought pressure upon those bound to obey it to participate in the antionchocerciasis campaign. As the National Campaign against Onchocerciasis gathers momentum it will doubtless augment and vary the role of local personnel.

Perhaps elements of indigenous Chinantec medical technology can be integrated into the program. Both the female nurse in the Yolox Health Center and the mobile brigade of male nurses who visit the more remote dependent hamlets make use of local people as guides, interpreters and general assistants. In Yolox perhaps the local medical specialists may assume some paramedical responsibilities. Massage is already a traditional technique in indigenous Chinantec medicine. Palpation for nodules appears to be a closely allied procedure and perhaps local specialists could participate in this diagnostic phase.

All indigenous medical specialists are mature persons, an asset of some importance where decision-making is largely the prerogative of mature or senior persons. Utilization of mature local personnel will have the additional advantage of minimizing gossip as a retarding factor in the success of the program. At least one local girl who had acquired some paramedical training under the nurse at the Yolox Health Center was compelled to abandon this work at the insistence of her father. Indigenous enterprises are traditionally hindered by the brisk clandestine rumor trade. Official attention has been called to the adverse effect upon the Campaign of malicious gossip (Ortiz Mariotte 1963:12).

The most serious consequence of blindness in this marginal society is the loss of the ability to do adult labor. As filarial blindness generally occurs late in life, most blind men have passed the age when they would normally be liable for *tequio,* the communal assessment of days of labor upon male youths and adults below the age of sixty-two. Though old age is a period of relative leisure and ripe judgment, it is not formal retirement but a time of diminished participation in the family subsistence regime. The lady generally singled out as the oldest woman in the village was unable to make the arduous descent to the ranchos, but she tended the fowl of another village family, leaving them free to travel. A number of senior women maintain the family High Village house, caring for children in school while most of the able-bodied members work the rancho plots.

Much of the declining tradition of domestic manufacture is in the hands of senior men. The weaving of hats and baskets, the twining of cargo nets, the carving of *canoas* (large wooden storage containers) and the production of gourd drinking and storage containers occupy time formerly devoted to the more rigorous requirements of subsistence activity.

Blindness, however, forces a more drastic retirement. Both blind and sighted villagers generally describe blindness as completely incapacitating. The most extreme poverty and dependence are thought to be "natural" states for blind persons. To be "poor as a blind man" is to be in as wretched an economic state as local imagination can conceive. They are "always led by the hand." This abject image, while valid in the main, is substantially qualified by individual cases. Three blind men have retained the skill of twining cargo nets. The sale of these nets and the yields of their coffee trees maintain these three blind men and their households at above median subsistence level. Failure to approximate closely the customary expectations exposes the blind, as it does any other person, to suspicion and negative criticism. But the majority of blind persons who do conform rather closely to those expectations are subject to still another kind of negative attitude. "They will say 'that *cabrón* (old goat) is blind, why is he not poor?' and if he is poor they will become angry if the blind man asks them for a little charity" (H. T. F. Field Notes).

However, as "God's afflicted," the blind are customarily entitled to public courtesy and the actual patterns of interaction between blind and sighted villagers approximates very closely this ideal. There is a pronounced decrease in malicious gossip about blind persons and their public "abuses" are treated with far less severity than the same offenses committed by sighted villagers.

When Don Rafael made himself drunk after much drinking and abused some of the people with many hard words and even struck some with his sticks, it was a bad thing. But the Authority did not make him pay a multa *as they would if he*

*were a sound man. They spoke mildly to him and he answered
them softly and no one spoke of it very much after that for we
were all ashamed.*   [C. H. D. FIELD NOTES]

Blind informants frequently characterized their sighted
paisanos as "stingy" while sighted villagers expressed re-
sentment at the demands of blind paisanos. But both the
sighted and the blind were reluctant and guarded in the
expression of these negative opinions.

The widespread belief that the blind are under special
divine protection appears to be instrumental in the
strength of the deference generally accorded them. They
are said to be protected against the bite of venomous
reptiles and the shock of lightning. They are assured a
long, if not especially happy life. God prevents them from
falling into the deep chasms which flank the principal
tracks of the municipio and has inspired a "natural" desire to serve them in the hearts of their paisanos, especially in the hearts of young children.

Sorting coffee beans without sight.

Blind persons of both sexes take sporadic part in the household tasks. Women work a little at the metate and an elderly blind woman joins the village women with her laundry at the *chorro* (spring) upon occasion. Blind men select especially fine maize ears for seed and sort coffee beans. Blind men are sometimes encountered pulling weeds in the fields, especially in cane patches where the several varieties of weed are distinguishable by touch from the useful plant. Sighted villagers do not place much practical value on this work but consider its chief worth to be the sense of usefulness it inspires in the individual blind person. Quite apart from its obvious economic value, the ability to perform adult labor is vital to the sense of self-esteem of most villagers.

Mendicancy, however, more especially the begging expedition, is an activity from which most blind villagers derive a great sense of approved, purposeful participation in the life of their pueblo. All the blind of Yolox have begged and most still do. Local, extramunicipal mendicancy is the preferred form but blind Yoleño beggars, especially women, do ask charity within the village. Blind men tend to adhere more closely to the mild village opposition to regular begging within the village. They beg furthest afield, some having traveled as far as Veracruz and even the national capital. Blind village women tend to mount less ambitious, more localized begging expeditions and to respect a great deal less the negative attitude toward regular intravillage begging.

Village bounty consists almost exclusively of small donations of food. A beggar is either invited to share a meal or a few tortillas are placed in the basket which is carried to receive such donations. On the rare occasions when money is given, the gift is small, rarely more than a half peso.

The extremely broken terrain of the municipio makes unaided travel by a blind person extremely difficult and often hazardous. On begging expeditions and conventional travel they rely almost exclusively upon the assistance of child guides. One of the major social consequences of onchocerciasis has been the amplification of the relationship between two groups at either extremity of the life course. The role of Lázaro is well established among village children. Adults act more rarely as guides but villagers look upon the service as being mutually beneficial and especially appropriate when rendered by young children. The importance of child guides is enhanced by the absence of nonhuman guides. Villagers regard the service by children as "natural" and are quick to characterize the reliance upon nonhuman guides as unnatural and repugnant. Child guides accompany blind men and women on begging expeditions both local and distant. The blind attend village fiestas with even greater frequency than sighted Yoleños and much of this diversion time is spent with children.

Child guides say they learn to perform their service by observing more experienced persons. Children do not call themselves guides nor do they generally refer to their services as guiding. A game of marbles, a storytelling session, an impromptu street interview was frequently prematurely but politely broken off as one or more of my younger friends and informants dashed off to "walk" with one of the village blind persons. My first young informant was a ten-year-old who was delegated by many of her playfellows to ask me if I wished "to walk with the children of the village as Don Manuel and Don Cipriano did."

An indispensable element in the easy rapport which characterizes relations between child guide and adult blind in Yolox is the shared nonmetaphysical concept concerning blindness. The environment is so manifestly inimical to unaided travel that all villagers regard such travel by blind persons as dangerous folly. Village children regard the physical dependence of their blind elders as a necessary physical consequence of blindness. Yoleño culture attempts neither to minimize nor to isolate the blind individual. Expressions of pity are, in many circumstances, quite in order and blind persons themselves are expected to enlarge upon the disadvantages of their handicap. Even superficial amity implies a great deal of commiseration for the misfortune of one's fellow villagers. A friend is quite literally "one who feels your grief." Many informants of both sexes were moved to tears by their narration of their own sad autobiographies. Though blind and sighted villagers make guarded, private accusations of undue parsimony and excessive mendicancy, no sighted Yoleño ever complained about the demands of their blind paisanos upon their time and empathy.

The mild, patient indulgence which village adults display toward young children and the strong desire to "be useful" are weighty factors in this transgenerational partnership. Most young children say they walk with the blind "out of love." Blindness as a negative possibility is as firmly established in the roster of juvenile negative expectations as it is in the adverse anticipations of village adults. There is a paucity of surface manifestations of the anxiety occasioned by blindness and the other elements of the village catastrophic precedents. The same defensive jocularity which village adults reserve for discussing "our fleas," "our poverty," "our blindness" is observable in the daily behavior of children. Most of the village children who came to offer to walk with me or to make a connoisseur's judgment upon the several varieties of hard candy which had survived the trip from Oaxaca City would preface their magnanimity with a well-worn riddle. In response to the question "Who is the patron of this place?" I always managed to reply "Saint Peter." I would then be assured that the true patron was Saint Martin. *"San Martín de Porres?"* I would ask quizzically. Then my small guest would say, "No, Don Juan, our patron is *San Martín de Pobres!"* (Saint Martin of the Poor.)

The children walk with the blind "out of love."

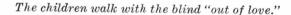

Anxiety about blindness was sometimes observable in casual play. "When we were playing at breaking the piñata, I was thinking what a pity it would be if God closed our eyes while they were covered" (R. H. P. Field Notes).

Blindness figures with varying frequency in the dreaming of many children. The inability to remove a blindfold after a game, the failure of vision which makes it impossible for the dreamer to alert his family to impending danger or transitory opportunity, and the reversal of role in the "child guide—adult blind" relationship were recurrent ominous themes.

If you are lucky you will have a good life. You will play for a long time as a child and never cry for bread. You will go about your father's lands like an important young man should and your parents will find a girl for you who is mild, obedient and well made. And there will come many children, many strong, intelligent sons and perhaps an obedient daughter. If you are as lucky as most men you will cry because you are empty and you will play but a short time. Then you will walk up and down seeking a space between the stones to sow the corn that stops the mouth of hunger. [H. P. FIELD NOTES]

PREGNANCY

Yoleños consider pregnancy to be the natural consequence of cumulative copulation. Young men who enjoy a relationship of extreme amity speculate that pregnancy might occur as a result of a single copulation but as a general rule the belief that pregnancy is the result of continual coitus appears to be firmly established.

The marginality of village life notwithstanding, a large family is regarded as a desirable end of any of the culturally approved forms of permanent sexual union. Ideally, large families with a preponderance of male off- spring are preferred. The reason most often advanced for this preference is the approximation of the single most-esteemed state in the Yoleño value scheme, familial self-sufficiency. In the ideal family projected by all in- formants many sons to work the family parcels was invariably a priority element.

As Don P., an aged blind man who had been obliged to flee his home in the Yoleño colony of Las Bocas because of involvement in a particularly bitter land feud, put it: "Here we have nothing! My two sons work for nothing to feed me. And if I had no sons, how then should I eat?" (B. P. Field Notes.) He further declared that the principal reason why his old age was as "bitter" as it was was the lamentable fact that he had only two sons. As it was, the support of his sons kept him from having to beg. Don P. was one of the few blind persons in the municipio who expressed a very strong aversion to mendicancy.

As in most areas of speculation, Yoleños are pretty much bound by the real imperatives of their own situ- ation. Abstract fantasying of an extravagant kind is unsettling or ludicrous to most villagers. Questions in- volving this kind of thinking were almost always difficult to grasp without a fairly lengthy mutual exchange of clarifying discourse. People projected the best practically conceivable family unit which might naturally occur among men and women who were in most respects like themselves.

Sterility is looked upon as a particularly grievous stroke of fortune. All informants questioned esteemed a childless marriage a less tolerable one than a union which produced only female offspring. A middle-aged childless couple were mentioned frequently when villagers were asked to name those of their neighbors who had been dealt especially hard fates. Their plight was evaluated almost as negatively as widowhood. They were generally referred to as *"los secos"* (the dry ones), and some blind persons considered that this couple's "cross" was as heavy as their own.

Sterility is thought to occur in both males and females but females are thought to be far more liable than males to this particular misfortune. A number of circumstances are thought of as being instrumental in its development. Witchcraft on the part of a woman's mother-in-law or a rival for her husband's affections is a very infrequently mentioned possibility. The excessive indulgence of a taste for extremely "cold" foods on the part of women, especially the pulp and juice of a wild lemon and the flesh of herbivorous game is sometimes held to be at fault.

Severe sustos, grave trauma-producing shocks to the system occasioned by extreme fear or anger or prolonged exposure to inclement weather or violence, are thought of as producing a number of severe pathological reactions. Mental illness, speech defects and barrenness are often attributed to the agency of susto. Thus a president of the municipio is believed to have contracted diabetes because of a severe susto which he sustained as a result of his detention in the Oaxaca jail during the official investigation of the most serious recent clash in the bloody land feuding between San Pedro Yolox and the neighboring municipio of Santiago Comaltepec. These possible causes of infertility are all secondary. Don H. P., replying to my question about the reason why a couple was "seco" after many years of marriage answered, "Why? who knows why! God willed it, that's all!"

In a phrase, the greatest single cause of sterility and all other misfortunes is divine caprice. Fate, the manifestation of God's will, strikes some and spares others and neither God's purposes nor His powers can be called into account by mere men. Whatever God wills is good, or if not good, surely unalterable.

None of the methods of birth control of the greater Mexican medical tradition have made any significant impact on the municipio. Not one of that small group of young men who, by virtue of their acquaintance with Oaxaca City, Tuxtepec and other urban centers, enjoy a reputation for worldly sagacity, had ever seen any contraceptive device. Indeed, the leader of this worldly wing, a young man whose carnal savoir faire was attested to by his proud possession of the only subscription to *Playboy* magazine in the community, was similarly uninformed. No kind of contraceptive device could be purchased in any of the stores of the village.

The ideal set of attitudes notwithstanding, pregnancy is often an inopportune state and women do, in actual fact, have recourse to a number of abortive procedures. There is at least one wild herb in the Yoleño folk pharmacopoeia which is brewed to make a tea which is widely thought to be inducive of abortion. The flesh of the armadillo and the juices of certain citrus fruits are reputed to produce abortion when consumed in great quantity because of their excessive "coldness."

Pregnant women are ideally supposed to display a general demeanor of diffident modesty. A kind of girlish shyness is deemed highly appropriate. Any other public demeanor is likely to call down charges of unnaturalness and earn the hapless offender the unenviable reputation of a *sin vergüenza,* a title roughly equivalent to the Victorian "shameless hussy." The culture demands that pregnant women be quite literally *"embarasada."* * It is a tribute of massive dimension to their ingenuity and monumental patience that most women, often those who have had multiple confrontations with what is, after all, one of the most regularly recurrent and perilous crises in the society, do maintain the public appearance of chagrin. Needless to say, the passage of time renders this public posture increasingly perfunctory.

The vital role played by its feminine members in maintaining the family as an autonomous subsistence unit precludes any protracted seclusion of women during pregnancy. In the latter stages women may in some cases be spelled at the metate by a woman hired to do some of the milling. For most women, however, childbearing does not involve any suspension of work but simply means that it must be performed under more wearying and disadvantageous conditions. The attitude of one informant who referred to pregnancy as "just another cross" seems to be fairly representative.

Birth takes place at home. There are two professional midwives in the village. There is also a nurse at the newly constructed Health Center who could also attend at births. Pregnant women, especially those bearing their first child, are supposed to rely heavily upon the experience and guidance of their mothers-in-law.

A number of folk remedies are employed to facilitate

* The common Spanish word for pregnancy in general use among the Chinantec is *embarrassed.*

the recovery of the mother. An herb called *chamiso blanco* is heated with the smoke of resinous pine. The treated herb is then tied around the waist of the new mother. This remedy is employed in from two to five days after the woman has given birth. This remedy with smoke-treated chamiso is said to be all but universally employed. A garland of avocado leaves is sometimes placed on the breasts of women who have recently given birth to facilitate the flow of milk. A strength-giving potion made of the crumpled dried leaves of chamiso blanco which have been mixed with hot mescal is given to the convalescent woman on the first, tenth and twentieth day after delivery. The much more potent locally distilled crude rum called *chingare* is sometimes substituted for mescal in the preparation of this general fortifying remedy. On the tenth day after delivery the new mother is expected to rise and prepare ten tortillas. It is believed that her face will swell if she makes any more than ten. Ideally people speak of a month of recovery but the rising on the tenth day already marks the reentry of the new mother into the work regime.

An ostentatiously displayed ignorance of the details of the delicate condition is considered an indispensable element of fully efficient masculinity. No male subject wished to be cast in the role of knowledgeable informant on this particular area of life. Women are thought to be weaker in physical strength and reasoning capacity under normal circumstances. Men say that they know that this inferiority is augmented by a woman's "being embarrassed." They expect that it will take a pregnant woman longer to organize and perform the household tasks.

The public posture in all areas of intersexual relationships is invariably overdrawn. Midwifery is woman's work so men are largely uninformed about it. Pregnancy is regarded as a woman's crisis, hence nothing that a man can be properly knowledgeable about. However, within the privacy of his own family unit, the individual male is more knowledgeable about pregnancy than he can admit publicly. As rapport took on the more profound aspects of friendship, veterans of marriage who had, upon initial questioning, professed complete ignorance about pregnancy observances and customs began to remember how to make the tea from the leaves of the plant called *aire* which relaxes pregnant women.

The making of cradles is man's work in Yolox. Every father has an obligation to provide a cradle fashioned of bent poles and coarsely woven netting. It is a man's duty to make and suspend the cradle from the ceiling rafters of his house with his own hands and his public estimation would suffer a severe decline if he neglected this duty for any but the most compelling reasons.

INFANCY

I was born into this world and I lived. And I grew in under-standing little by little. And as soon as I began to understand a few words, I began to want things. I would say to my father, Papa, I want this thing or that thing or some other thing. But my father would always say, how can I get it for you and who will bring it to us?   [P. L. F. FIELD NOTES]

The most striking and readily apparent difference between Yoleño babies and other infants known to me is plainly measurable in decibels. The Yoleño infant is quieter. It was very often extremely difficult for me to detect the presence of a waking child in a one-room house during a visit of an hour's duration or more, a circumstance which I failed to find in my extensive exposure to North American infants.

A second noticeable difference is that of the degree of activity. A child of from six to eight months of age will lie for protracted periods in a net cradle suspended from the ceiling rafters of the house without setting the free-swinging cradle in motion.

Oddly enough, the states of the very young infant and the elderly blind are often regarded as analogous. Passivity is thought to be a necessary condition of both estates. A state of quiescence is thought of as the best one for the infant's adjustment to "this world." This world is fraught with a number of perils for the newly arrived.

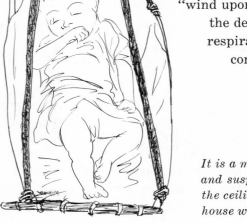

A host of malignant agencies, natural and supernatural, lay unremitting siege to the young child's flesh and spirit. Measles, "wind upon the stomach" and the deadly assemblage of respiratory furies known commonly as "cough"

It is a man's duty to make and suspend the cradle from the ceiling rafters of his house with his own hands.

may very well carry him off. Older people still speak reluctantly of *los aires,* testy sprites who must be propitiated to avoid their ready malice. But generally this peevish assemblage is referred to as *el aire* and may or may not be personified, depending upon the "progressiveness" of the individual informant.

The most progressive local view is that el aire is a natural condition in the atmosphere which may weaken the young child if it is not guarded against. There are a number of informants who, in prolonged conversation about el aire or los aires, slip back and forth between the singular and plural form and who refer to this condition or agency alternately as being impersonal and personified.

The most general defense against el aire is to keep the head of the infant covered. This is the practice in families of all economic levels. The covering might vary from a cap acquired expressly for a particular young child to a well-worn cotton or wool hat which has obviously seen service many times.

Whatever the thinking about the natural or supernatural status of aire there is common agreement about the necessity of maintaining a general air of placidity. Here too, as in many other aspects of life, it is the exposure to the unconventional which is looked upon as being especially traumatic. The wife of B. M. looked upon an eclipse of the moon while pregnant. She knows that is why her child died soon after birth. There is also general accord on the instrumentality of the will of Heaven in infant mortality. An infant might possibly incur a mortal dose of divine wrath or retributive ire for some offense of one of his parents, especially some grievous paternal tort. Considerations of sin quite aside, it might please the Deity to take the life of a child for any reason. "It may please Him to do whatever He is pleased to do."

Almost all Yoleño babies are breast fed. If the mother is unable to give the breast another lactating woman is asked to feed the child. This is one of the few services for which no payment may properly be demanded. There is an almost total dependence upon mother's milk on the part of nonambulatory infants. *Biberones* (rubber nipples) are available at 1 peso each in the stores of the High Village. The baby bottle had not put in an appearance in Yolox at the time of this writing. The rubber nipples are fitted to soda or beer bottles. Canned, condensed milk is also available and is sometimes used.

Women can obtain one bottle of powdered milk per day for each nursing infant in their family from the Health Center. More condensed milk is used as there is a strong prejudice against powdered milk. A third supply of milk, in this case, fresh whole milk, is sporadically available. Women occasionally walk in from neighboring pueblos to sell or barter cow's milk. Access to any of these secondary sources of milk is qualified by a number of circumstances. Pregnant women and those charged with the maintenance of preambulatory infants are obliged to move with their families in the round of shifting cultivation. When they are constrained to descend to the downslope hamlets, powdered milk is not available. Families are often obliged to spend months either below or above the central pueblo. The rugged nature of both the descending and ascending tracks force migrating families to travel as lightly as possible. Household goods and even the precious family fowl are often left in the care of older persons who must remain in the High Village. The carrying of a supply of canned milk sufficient to maintain even one nursing child for any length of time would prove an all but intolerable strain upon the backs and pocketbooks of most families.

Babies nurse from one and a half to three years. The length of time varies according to a number of considerations. Most people were of the opinion that girl children nurse longer because they are generally thought of as being more feeble. If the child is noticeably weak, even if it is ambulatory, it may continue to nurse. Most mothers say that they tend to "favor" boys in families where female offspring predominate.

Sometimes an attempt is made to introduce the nursing infant to the "food of men." There is a kind of tortilla called *memelita*. They are thick, round corn cakes well cooked on the outside but very soft inside. These small thick tortillas are soaked in very bland bean soup and fed bit by bit to the baby. While some families do attempt to acquaint the child with solid food in the latter part of the nursing period, the break with mother's milk and the introduction of solid food is more often than not an abrupt change. The nurse who administers the Health Center was of the opinion that this sudden transition from mother's milk to solid food is one of the major factors in infant mortality.

Infants' dress reflects differences in wealth. Extremely marginal families often wrap babies in cast-off adult clothing. Thus an undershirt which is too ragged even for the necessarily flexible taste of an adult will be pressed into the service of the youngest member of the family. There is a sewing machine in the largest of the four stores in the high pueblo and some women rent it in order to make infant's clothing and fiesta dresses. The most wealthy families bring in infant's clothing ordered from Oaxaca City. However the baby is dressed his clothing is viewed as having two main functions. It is often uncomfortably cold in even the most well-constructed dwelling at the level of the high ceremonial village. Infants are said to be especially in need of protection against this moist, biting cold.

Clothing is also thought of as defining the scope of the baby's motion. A ten-year-old girl informant and confidante who was a seasoned veteran of infant care put it this way. "A *rebozo* (shawl) is a little house for babies." No matter how many garments the baby may wear, the invariable outer garment is the firmly wrapped rebozo. When carried abroad or lying in his string cradle or tended by an older sibling, the child lives in the small tent that is some family member's rebozo. The baby's extremities, especially his legs, are limited by the encircling shawl as they are also within the folds of the rebozo. The one portion of the child's anatomy which is of necessity free is invariably covered with a cap of some kind to fend off the malicious attentions of el aire or los aires. The child is not so much bound in a literal sense but rather more limited.

The child is thus circumscribed, free to move with relative facility within the "little house" of the enveloping rebozo but generally not free to go very far beyond it. Even if the actual loosely enveloping garment is only an old undershirt, if it is the outermost article, it must shelter and circumscribe as the rebozo does.

Most of the practices of Yoleño child rearing work together to maintain that state of placidity deemed vital for the proper development of the infant into a young child.

Infancy, then, is a period of anxious anticipation for parents. The best evidence that the baby is successfully negotiating the narrow, peril-studded passage is the absence of the extraordinary. The development of the child is thought of as a feeble and surreptitious progression through a morass of manifold dangers. It is a wary, wearying journey which does not end until the feet of the small traveler are planted firmly on the hard-packed earthen floor of the house in which he was born, and he has quit the breast which sustained him all that long, dangerous way for "the food of men."

CHILDHOOD

When I was seven I went to school. My brother and my sister and I went and we were very poor. Then a pencil was a precious thing to be broken into three parts. Then my little sister died and we broke them only in two parts.   [P. M. FIELD NOTES]

Childhood is a time of easy tutelage for the youngster who has quit the breast, learned to walk, and is able to leave the family patio to defecate and urinate. All three of these accomplishments of early childhood are generally mastered by the third year of the child's existence. Of the three, weaning is by far the most abrupt. The first food commonly substituted for mother's milk is *atole de maiz,* a kind of sweetened cornstarch. Oatmeal is available in one of the stores of the village and is sometimes purchased for the preparation of *atole de avena,* a very thin oatmeal gruel which is also used during the transition from milk to the food of men. Weaning is accomplished by the gradual retiring of the mother. Her place is taken by the mother-in-law who feeds the child atole of one kind or another spoonful by patient spoonful as the child indicates hunger by restlessness or crying. Should the mother-in-law for any reason be unable to perform this duty, one of the neighbor women is hired for about 2 pesos a night. There is an extreme prejudice against having this service performed by the maternal grandmother. The nurse at the Health Center says that this is never done. No informant could ever remember a case of a maternal grandmother acting in this capacity.

As the first critical stages of earliest infancy are passed, an ever-increasing responsibility for the daytime care of the youngster falls upon the older children of the household, more especially upon the older girls of the family. Thus it is that the first adult responsibility falls upon little girls among Yoleños.

Most informants say that it normally requires four days to make the dietary transition. By the time weaning procedures are initiated, junior females are able to take almost complete responsibility for the daytime care of the young child.

In opposition to the rather precipitous weaning process the Yoleño child learns to walk pretty much at his own somewhat leisurely pace. He is not encouraged to adopt this new mode of locomotion. He appears to make more than the usual number of abortive attempts. When these fail he is patiently reinstalled within the security of the sheltering shawl, placed against some familiar shoulder and there gathers strength for the next assay.

No intense effort is made to persuade the child to make another attempt at walking. His attempts are viewed with mild interest and his failures greeted with an amalgam of self-conscious humor and exaggerated concern. The length of the periods of placidity are gradually reduced. The reduction is not a steady progression but a general diminution of reliance upon the security of his string cradle or the rebozo. The child spends more time on the floor. Elder siblings, generally sisters, keep the child within the prescribed area of safety on the hard-packed earthen house floor.

The young child learns to relate safely to the hearth and to avoid the pitchpine torch or beer-can petroleum lamp which are the all but universal sources of light. Largely under the patient, protective tutelage of their mothers and those "little mothers," their elder sisters, children learn reverence for the family altar, or that portion of the house where religious articles are prominently displayed. They "show respect for the house" by learning not to defecate or urinate within the confines of the house.

The pace at which the young child masters the subtle, homonym-laden, synonym-rich Chinantec language is also left largely to his own inclination. The attempts of the very young to cope with its manifold minute distinctions often occasion considerable innocent merriment and similar efforts on the part of at least one graduate anthropologist often led to fully efficient hilarity.

It is considered a major breach of form deliberately to confuse a child. During the day mothers and the guardian sisters patiently perfect the child's rough approximation of "correct Chinanteco." A child is rarely subjected to even the mildest ridicule at this stage. Fathers and older brothers returned from a day's labor in the fields will also talk with the child occasionally. Irascibility toward a child of this age is considered extremely barbarous be-

The acquisition of sierra legs is a relatively rapid process.

havior so these exchanges are carried forward in a patient humorous vein. Yolox is a difficult place for a child to learn to walk in. All of its streets are extremely steep with many steps which exceed the child's height. Beyond the special protective environment of their respective house sites in the custody of older siblings, falls are inevitable. Only the mildest exhortations to walk are given the child. The nature of their broken terrain and the necessities of subsistence require that Yoleños be indefatigable walkers. The first lesson in acquiring this endurance is the trip to a latrine area with an older brother or sister. The young child is often taken along on trips to the nearer commons to gather kindling or goes to the spring for the family supply of drinking water. Young children accompany their mothers to the common laundry areas and scramble up and down the steep slope while the women exchange pleasantries and gossip at the concrete washing basins. Once seriously begun the acquisition of sierra legs is a relatively rapid process. A blind informant was led over several kilometers of extremely rugged, rolling country on numerous local begging expeditions by a young granddaughter who was not yet five. A six-year-old girl guide led Doña V., an elderly blind woman, considerable distances to interviews and on local begging trips.

The Chinantec of Yolox believe that there is a natural antagonism between boys and girls which manifests itself most violently around the ages of six or seven. When asked why boys and girls were seated separately in the village school most people expressed the opinion that they would quarrel or even fight if they were not segregated.

Young children but recently freed from the protective confinement of their house sites by the acquisition of increasing mobility play together. It is this period of relatively free exploration that adults look back on with nostalgia. Then children are as free from the pressing cares of subsistence as they will ever be. "My older sons

Several lengths of bamboo are
fashioned into a toy gun.

help to cut coffee, but the little ones do nothing but play and ask for food." There are clay marbles, balloons, and a variety of rubber balls available in the stores. But the price of such toys brought in from Oaxaca City puts them beyond the regular access of very many families. A bit of string, a bottle top, the dried peel of a fruit, or a length of bamboo, all are transformed by the imagination of the young, and not infrequently the addition of a little adult expertise, from rubbish to absorbing toys.

A piece of string and the thick-stemmed waxy skinned half of a dried citrus fruit (*limón de aire*) becomes a durable and highly maneuverable spinning top. Soda-bottle tops are coveted as casseroles in the season of mud cookery which flourishes between the termination of the heavy autumnal rains and the inception of the dry sunny winter. Tops of mineral water bottles and the caps of a certain ubiquitous North American soft drink serve as pieces for games which divert both young and old. Youngsters hoard these bottle caps and imitate the soldiers playing at checkers. Several lengths of bamboo are fashioned into a toy gun which hurls stones or sticks.

Children of this age do not indulge in very many competitive play activities. Basketball and volleyball are imports which are increasing in popularity among teen-aged children with school affiliations. Both baseball and soccer have a small spectator following but these sports are elements of the greater Mexican tradition and their progress is noted only by the occasional newspaper or radio relation. There is simply not enough level ground to play either of these games in the village.

Indigenous play is relatively free from a strong competitive spirit. Little boys are not anxious to be more accomplished top spinners than their fellows. The terrain and the inclination of the culture militate against foot races. Children are occasionally permitted to ride the family burro for a short time purely for the pleasure of the experience, but I never witnessed nor could discover any informant who could recall children racing each other on these animals.

Even during the great fiesta of the fifteenth of January, when young men and youths attempt to ride the bulls which have been recently corralled after months of free grazing, the only competition is between rider and animal. No attempt is made to ascertain which of the contestants remained mounted the longest. No one is singled out because of his skill and no man or boy is criticized because of his lack of prowess. Contestants ride for the fiesta, not against each other. Young children appear a great deal more preoccupied with the cooperative activity of a given game than with excelling as individuals.

Children's play is also in considerable degree instructive and preparatory. Much of it is concerned with the inculcation of attitudes and acquisition of skills which characterize the respective sexual roles which must be learned if girls and boys are to become responsible women and men. Much play activity is in actual fact centered on a genuine work situation. Younger children may be permitted to accompany their older siblings to the commons to gather kindling or to the spring for water. The younger children gather smaller bundles of wood and carry small cans full of water. It is a privilege for the small girl to fashion small tortillas of dubious cleanliness on the edge of the metate on which her mother or elder sister is preparing the family's supply of corn cakes.

Play activity becomes increasingly dichotomized as boys and girls settle into their respective sexual roles. As children mature the more closely their play approximates real participation in the actual functioning of the family as an economic unit. And the closer play approximates real participation in family economy the greater is the reflection of the sexual division of labor. By the age of five or six younger brothers begin to follow their slightly older male siblings and girls of five or six are increasingly homebound as are their older sisters.

By the time the young boy is seven he can be entrusted with the midday meal which is often delivered to those members of the family working in the fields. The young boy spends an ever-increasing amount of his time in the company of his older male kin observing them performing "men's work." The time at which a boy actually joins his father in useful field tasks varies with the economic circumstances of his family. Families in more favorable economic circumstances are in a position to hire more field labor and hence are able to delay the intense agricultural apprenticeship of their sons. Such families are likely to place a higher value upon formal education and maintain their children in the village school for a longer period than less-advantaged families. The extreme marginality of most Yoleño families obliges them to regard school as a luxury and to coopt their children into the subsistence activity of the family as soon as physiologically possible.

By the ninth birthday the average Yoleño child is well integrated into his family's subsistence regime. Girls are generally first to be seriously included in the family's adult work activity. Propriety dictates that they should be more closely observed and supervised than their broth-

ers. They are more directly under the immediate supervision of their mother. If the mother goes abroad some
young child, generally a girl, almost invariably accom-
panies her. At first the child fulfills the cultural requirement that women should not provoke gossip by permitting
themselves to be seen alone in public. As the girl grows
older she ceases to be just a gossip rod and performs with
increasing facility the many tasks of women and begins
to acquire the complex of attitudes subsumed in the concept of *vergüenza*. *Vergüenza* is, in its broadest sense, an
attitude of seemly modesty. Prudence appears to be at
least as instrumental in its preservation as conviction. Its
absence is looked upon as capital shamelessness. As little
girls begin to learn and sense this attitude from their
mothers and as their brothers begin to detect and learn
patterns of male dominance, their play becomes increasingly segregated along sexual lines. The easy bisexual
comradeship begins giving way to attitudes of mild mutual
scorn and general antagonism. Young boys observe and
imitate expected masculine patterns of behavior from their
elder brothers and their father. Tagging along with gangs
of older boys, tracking the family stock with an older
brother, watching his father and elder brothers cut coffee
or plod behind the plow, carefully noting the spicy Spanish which the young men lavish upon mules of all degrees
of recalcitrance—by these and innumerable instructive
occasions of exposure to men at work, men at play, men
in mild ribaldry and men observing the formalized strictures of a relationship of respect, the Yoleño boy learns
what his paisanos expect of him in the way of "man's
work" and masculine patterns of thought and behavior.
    It is this transformation from relatively undifferen-

tiated early childhood patterns of behavior and thinking to firmly established sexually dichotomized behavior and attitude patterns and not the onset of puberty that the culture takes note of and celebrates.

I said to my father, here among the Chinantec I can do nothing to make our misfortune less heavy. Let me go to school beyond this poor place. My father said no. You know we are obliged to serve the pueblo. When I am called to serve in the Ayuntamiento, *who will do the work of the family?*

[C. F. FIELD NOTES]

The older children grow the more difficult it is for them to engage in meaningful communication with their parents. The formal patterns of respect which become more firmly fixed with increasing maturity and the ascription of negative values to the airing of sexual matters in heterosexual or transgenerational company renders any conversation about the physiological alterations attendant upon sexual maturity generally brief, guarded, uneasy and uninformative. The most voluble, if not the most veracious, sources of satisfaction for such curiosity are older siblings. There the onus of respect is less rigorous. The talk of young men on the trail of their wandering stock, or an occasional intimate conversation with an older brother in the Single Men's Society go a long way toward assuaging the concern of a recently pubescent boy about the physiological changes he is experiencing.

Menstruating girls traditionally are supposed to be informed about the menses by their mothers. This enlight-

enment transpires in an atmosphere of clandestine con-
spiratorial chagrin when all males are absent from the
house. At the metate during the mother's absence with the
family laundry, while tending the family fowl on the trail
during one of the frequent shifts of residence, younger
sisters seize upon opportune occasions to persuade elder
sisters to enlarge upon the enlightenment.

Whatever anxieties are aroused by the onset of puberty
their resolution is not a culture-wide but a purely familial
responsibility. The real culture-wide test of maturity is
the capacity to perform adult labor. The society makes
provisions for training youths of both sexes who are on
the point of attaining to adulthood.

Boys generally join the Single Men's Society in their
fifteenth year. They do so by asking one of the two sacristans who advise and direct the Society to inscribe
their names on the roster. The Single Men's Society is
Yoleño culture's school for manhood. Its members learn
to give guarded expression to their opinions in its formal
meetings. They perfect themselves in the vital agrarian
skills on the parcels of land which the Society holds in
common. Membership introduces the young man to a set
of obligations and allegiances which foreshadow the demands which the pueblo makes of all its able-bodied
"sons." The Society obliges him to donate labor for the
sowing, cultivating and harvesting of societal plots. The
pueblo will exact a specified number of working days from
him for communal purposes. His age mates will saddle
him with some unsolicited responsibility. The assembled
male adults of his pueblo are free to bestow some pyrrhic
distinction upon him. He learns to yield with public good
grace to his parents' wishes, the suasion of his age mates

and the formidable will of his paisanos in lawful and awesome assembly.

The Single Men's Society is more than a school for drudgery and submission. It is also a band of comrades who are united by amity and common interests. At their ease in the sacristy adjoining the church, in groups at work on the societal land or in the juvenile sanctuary that is the "house of the single men" they share their strong drink, mildly expressed opinions and interminable gossip.

By the time a young man is ready to leave the Society for those statuses which he must hold before he is considered to be an adult, namely, those of husband and father, it has played an important part in his development. That segment of the process of cultural maturation has been overseen by four married men—two sacristans and the two *fiscales,* or treasurers of the Society. They are men of varying temperament. Some take their tutelage more seriously than others. Some are stricter in their observances of the conventions of the respect relationship than others. Some drink to excess while others are indifferent or abstemious. A young man keeps his own counsel and emulates that which he admires and rejects that which repels him. In the same guarded, introspective way he measures himself against his age mates in facility and diligence with the hoe, the machete, the draft animals and the Egyptian plow—those implements which are instrumental in the maintenance of most Yoleño families just above the minimal level of subsistence.

The presentation of some strong drink, generally mescal, to all his fellows symbolizes the departure of the young man from the Society. By the time he is twenty a young man's parents have probably selected a wife for him after some concession to his personal preferences. The youth's godfather of matrimony will have conducted the requisite negotiations.

There is also a rather more weakly developed institution for the instruction of girls in the attitudes and skills of adult women. The Single Women's Society possesses no communal land. Unlike the Single Men's Society it does not own a house of its own. In rare good times a fond father may set aside a small portion of the profit realized from the sale of his coffee crop for a particularly obedient daughter to donate to the treasury of the Single Women's Society. The Single Women's Society is complementary to the Single Men's Society. This ancillariness is far more pronounced in the relations between these two institutions than it is in actual day-to-day interaction between individuals of the two sexes. Within the limits of her own family circle the Yoleña may speak with a voice which approximates and, in some instances, surpasses in authority that of male kin. Maturity brings to women an increasing security and augments the generally perceptible degree of the perfunctory aspect of their culturally prescribed subordination.

But the Single Women's Society in its auxiliary role approximates the ideal patterns for interaction between the sexes. Both societies function to emphasize the respective roles of the two sexes. Chinantec society demands that a young woman be closely supervised by her own immediate kin until they surrender their rights as guardians to some other family through the contractual medium of matrimony. Interaction between the two societies reflects roughly the sexual division of labor which obtains in the families from which the youthful personnel are recruited and which they will perpetuate upon their attainment of adult status.

There is only one occasion when young women may properly be admitted to the house of the Single Men's Society. Then they come in a body and are extremely circumspect in their behavior. They are generally spoken for by the wives of the two sacristans who are the advisers of the Single Women's Society. On August fourteenth, on the eve of the celebration of the Feast of the Assumption which is the fiesta of the Single Men's Society youths of both sexes gather in the medium-sized adobe house of the Single Men's Society. The girls contribute whatever funds they have raised toward the cost of the fiesta.

The parcels of the Single Men's Society are given over to the cultivation of maize. The only exception is the tradition of sowing green beans amid the maize which are later distributed among the members of the Single Women's Society. The young men ask the sacristans to prevail upon their wives to ask the young ladies of the Single Women's Society to accept an invitation to attend their secondary harvest. The young ladies attend in a body and each of them receives a basket of the newly gathered green beans. Custom dictates that each girl make a meal of them for her family soon after the gift is presented or dry them for such a meal in the future. There is a most emphatic prohibition against the sale or donation of this gift.

The young men ask the sacristans to have their wives send the single girls to gather and cook *chilacallotas* for a general feast of white squash. The meal is cooked by the wives of the sacristans and fiscales with the assistance of the Single Women's Society. It is served by the wives of the sacristans. The members of the Single Men's Society eat it. There are always a few uninvited guests. Small boys who invite themselves are regarded as enterprising. Small girls who display the same initiative are thought to be shockingly deficient in that indispensable element of feminine character, vergüenza, maidenly chagrin. It is a rare girl who has not acquired sufficient vergüenza to render her impervious even to the formidable temptation of spiced, steamed squash by her seventh or eighth birthday. Needless to say, a pubescent girl could not secure parental permission to attend the Feast of White Squash, even if she were "shameless" enough to voice the request.

There is a feast of green corn in middle or late September. This meal is also cooked by the wives of the sacristans and fiscales with the assistance of the members of the Single Women's Society. It is also served to an all male company of single men who assemble for the occasion in the Society's house.

A young woman's stay in the Single Women's Society, though averagely more brief than the period of indoctrination and training of a young man, is no less obviously designed to pass on to her the skills and attitudes vital to her assumption of the role of an adult woman. Marriage comes earlier for girls. By the time she is sixteen, she will probably have left her parents' house for that of her husband's family; or, as frequently happens, a young man may have been brought into her family. Her indoctrination has been less elaborate, its course less regularized. It is at once less rigorous and less rewarding. The culture values it less highly than it does male indoctrination. It complements and supplements the family's efforts at indoctrination. It operates to make a young woman pri-

marily an efficient, modest junior partner in a conjugal
alliance. It serves to facilitate the transference of her
allegiance, deference and submission from parents to
spouse.

Only in the most peripheral sense can membership in
the Single Women's Society or the family for that matter
be said to prepare a young woman for wider responsibilities. Even allowing for Don F.'s admonition that "it is a
rare cook who dies of hunger," it is a fact that a young
woman is as effectively barred from formal participation
in the public affairs of the pueblo as she is from formal
attendance at the feasts of green corn and white squash
which she prepares.

MAJORITY

*When I was sixteen or seventeen I began to look for a wife
and when I was twenty I married. And then I had my children
—that's the way life is here!*   [B. R. Q. FIELD NOTES]

Irrespective of the reputation for diligence, restraint and
obedience a person of either sex may have acquired, the
pueblo does not confer the status of responsible adult before marriage and the birth of children.

Most informants agreed that a marriage is a contractual arrangement in which the pueblo takes official interest. An invitation to the entire municipal government
was once an expected element of every elaborate wedding.
Only five years ago at least one of the most affluent families observed this convention.

Majority, like most life states, is thought of as being
attained by degrees. Full adult status comes for a man

when he is a husband, a father, an independent director of the subsistence activity of a family unit and when he has begun to take an initial modest part in the round of official municipal service.

Whether the newly married couple lives in a new house or is domiciled with the parents of one or the other spouse it is generally subordinated to some senior family authority.

SENIORITY

My father didn't want to divide his property equally, but that was all right with me, I didn't want to beg him for anything, so the house is my brother's.   [W. J. C. FIELD NOTES]

So long as the senior parents can take a reasonably active part in the subsistence activity of the extended family they tend to have a dominant voice in the ordering of that regime. Fathers are extremely slow to relinquish title to the family parcels and make a division among their sons. The subordination of males is less readily apparent than that of female spouses. The husband is generally older at the time of marriage and is presumed to have learned his principal role of skilled farmer. He is more often than not in a subordinate relationship with his own kin. He is almost certain to have at least one powerful ally, his mother, who can be relied upon to minimize the clash of interests between those holding title to and those aspiring for possession of the plots upon which all depend for subsistence. Outside work requires less contact between senior and junior family personnel and often outdoor subsistence activity, especially in the very broken terrain of the municipio, requires that partners be separated by considerable distances for appreciable periods of time.

There is a generally held stereotype of the newly married female as an unskilled innocent whose only saving grace is her tractability. The mother-in-law is definitely viewed as a tutelary figure. Despite the more obvious subordination of the young bride, the very real disadvantage of being more often than not among her husband's kin and the tedium and propinquity of most female work, women of both generations maintain that surface amity which functions to facilitate most interpersonal relationships in Yolox.

Senior women are thought to be more tolerant with the shortcomings of their daughters-in-law than with those of their own daughters. In actual fact, however, most young women continue to perform those tasks peculiar to women in Yolox which they have learned under their own parental roof. The incapacity of the new bride is more apparent than real. The only area of adult experience in which the mother-in-law is generally more knowledgeable than her junior work mate is the realm of sexuality. Except for passing on the store of traditional lore and custom relative to pregnancy, sexuality is precluded as a fit subject of conversation between mother-in-law and daughter-in-law by the conventions of respect.

Sexuality in any of its aspects and the number and size of land parcels were the two subjects which informants of both sexes were most reluctant to discuss. Female virginity is esteemed but no formal proof of it is demanded at marriage.

If she survives the multiple perils of recurrent pregnancy, the birth and maturation of her own children and the gradual aging of her senior instructress confer first independence and then seniority upon the younger woman in the normal course of things.

With seniority comes a degree of personal autonomy which women do not enjoy at any other period in the life cycle. For women a sense of personal worth derives far less from the ability to perform adult labor than it does for men. The strictures of the several respect relationships are less confining than at any other period except early childhood.

An elderly blind informant was the first to voice an opinion which was general among elder men. "When a woman gets older she becomes more ignorant." As proof of this allegation older male informants would go on to recount instances in which their counsel or wishes had been ignored with varying degrees of indifference, often bordering on outright disrespect. Intractability is often regarded as synonymous with ignorance or even evil. Plainly what these gentlemen were deprecating was not stupidity but that good humored autonomy which is so often observed in the personalities of mature Yoleñas. The exclusion of women from any formal participation in the conduct of the political and ceremonial round of the pueblo fosters a variance between the attitudes of men and women. The reaction of women to their exclusion from formal participation is a jocular refusal to take public life and public questions quite as seriously as most men would like them to.

A cleavage analogous to that juvenile dichotomy between the sexes which sends boys and girls into differing play activity reoccurs with the attainment of seniority. Success for women is narrowly defined as synonymous with attainment of the status of senior directress of her own family. If they live long enough, most women will achieve something like this distinction. The even greater emersion of women in the affairs of their respective families leads to an even greater emphasis upon the primacy of family as opposed to community allegiance.

It is frequently necessary to divide the family. Often a senior woman will be left with minor children to tend the family stock and guard its upslope dwelling while younger women and able-bodied men may descend the slope to work the rancho parcels. This pattern is all but obligatory for the increasing minority of families which place a very high value upon formal education in the one school of the municipio. Such a division entails in many cases extreme privation, even by prevailing local standards. Thus it is that persons at both ends of the generational continuum are frequently obliged to endure protracted periods of extreme hunger together. Many informants spoke with great emotion of the selfless division of the meager food supply made by senior women. Grandmothers are figures of compassion. Many other informants displayed negative feelings of equal strength when recounting the treatment they were accorded by senior women outside their own family.

Marriage is the first step for a young man toward full adult status. Some years, however, must pass before he attains this prime position. It is not likely that he will be considered for any weighty public charge before he is also a father. As patrilocality is the dominant but by no means exclusive residence pattern, the chances are that he will continue to work the same land he has tilled since early youth. His work mates are likely to be his own kin and he will dwell in or near the house in which he was born. If he has joined a family which formerly consisted of a fictive widow and her offspring his lot is regarded as hard but more tolerable than joining the extended family of his bride. Whether matrilocal, uxorelocal or patrilocal, he will not be his own man until he is the recognized mainstay of his family's subsistence. He must await the often long-delayed decision of the senior personnel of the extended family to yield him a portion of the family's land and delegate him an equal share of authority in the higher councils of the minimal subsistence unit.

As he proceeds in slow stages from relative subordination through rough equity to possible dominance within his particular kin group he is also moving in the pueblo-wide official cycle.

His progress in the politico-ceremonial system is regulated by the assessment of his fellow married males. There are twenty-four positions to fill every year and the pueblo may thrust this often unwelcomed eminence upon any married male. However pyrrhic, the election of one's paisanos is an all but iron mandate.

The most successful

Old age is ideally a time of increased leisure.

senior males are those who have served their pueblo in every capacity from policeman to president and have risen to a dominant position within their particular family unit. True success, then, because of the wider area of attainment comes less frequently to senior males than it does to females who have achieved similar age. The attainment of seniority occasions a necessary decline in one of the pillars of a man's concept of personal worth, namely the ability to do adult labor.

Whatever disposition a senior male makes of his property, he is bound to displease at least one of his sons. This displeasure rarely finds overt expression. Whenever this disposition is made it seems unjustly delayed to those awaiting it. Senior males, then, are open to charges of undue parsimony and favoritism which, though unexpressed in face-to-face confrontations, still often preclude that warm relationship common between senior females and their juniors.

Seniority brings some satisfactions to both men and women. Old age is ideally a period of increased leisure. If a man has worked with reasonable diligence the pueblo will pity rather than criticize his retirement. Indeed, the society itself liberates him from any assessments of money or days of communal labor at the age of sixty-two.

Seniority brings with it a reputation for sagacity and mature discernment. The extensive involvement in the politico-ceremonial system enhances this reputation. And senior males find a measure of public prestige which compensates to some degree for the decline which old age occasions in some aspects of their most personal relationships.

Senior males often attempt to hold on to as much

domestic dominance as possible while enjoying the prestigious public status of principal or senior adviser. A number of informants speak of death-bed conferences at which the patriarch divides his property and holdings.

MORTALITY

I am seventy-two years old and if God gives me another year I'll be seventy-three. But if I don't have that good fortune there are other friends who will reach that age. I will tell you frankly, I have seen many years of life, and I have suffered greatly, compañero. *You might say my years are now beginning to weigh a little heavily upon me.* [V. L. G. FIELD NOTES]

The protracted prevalence of death in many forms has fostered a traditional reaction of apprehensive resignation. Yoleños are conscious of death as an omnipresent leveler. It is the instrument of a divinity whose salient attribute is power. Like most awe-inspiring uncontrollable phenomena, death does not generally figure largely in adult conversation. Young children follow funeral processions and occasionally play funerary games.

The only person who spoke of suicide was an old woman who had outlived all her kin and was alone and destitute. A major deterrent was the knowledge that taking her own life was, according to the canons of Roman Catholicism, a sin for which she might be punished by eternal separation from her kin in the other world.

All deaths should ideally be registered with the Authority in the ceremonial village and a formal cause of death properly noted. Some deaths are eventually registered and formal causes of death set down with Elizabethan imprecision. The Authority also levies a tax of communal labor upon all able-bodied males to maintain in good repair the low, rough rock wall which surrounds the small cemetery in the High Village.

With the exception of the registration of deaths and the maintenance of burial grounds, death is not a matter of general public concern. An individual's death is his family's concern. There are no formal funeral specialists. The family of the deceased purchase the cloth for the *mortaja*, the formal garment of interment. The adult dead are bathed and clad in a shroud of "serious" colors: black, white, purple, or navy blue. Grave clothes are essentially the same for both sexes. Women may be interred in figured mortajas so long as there is no departure from the traditional serious colors.

Children are clad in the same long nightshirt-like garment. But serious colors are inappropriate for dead children. White or sky blue are said to be the most fitting colors for their grave clothes. The funerals of children are occasions for far less solemnity than are the last rites for adults as baptized children are thought of as being assured of a place in paradise.

Coffins are sometimes used but corpses are commonly wrapped and tied in a straw sleeping mat. The face is covered with a rebozo and the deceased is borne to the grave upon a crude bier fashioned of two long parallel poles joined with cross-slats which is thrown away after use.

The dead are thought of as maintaining an interest in the pueblo. They are stern punitive figures with whom the most rigorous respect relationships must be maintained. They are thought to be possessed of the same personalities in the next life which they displayed in "this world."

The pueblo certainly maintains a lively interest in the dead. The living expect their dead paisanos to inform them through dreams and visions about the future and to act as intercessors before the saints or God Himself. This link between the living and the dead is manifested in the formidable economic outlay it occasions in propitiatory, sentimental, commemorative sacred observances. Of all masses purchased services for the dead preponderate.

THE ROLE OF NEGATIVE EXPECTATIONS
IN VILLAGE CHARACTER

*I shall live as long as I shall live. So I don't want anyone
to eat mushrooms or cast beans for me. It pleased God to give
me this long sad life. His snakes did not kill me and His
lightning did not destroy me, but my eyes have been closed
for two years now.* [B. H. Q. FIELD NOTES]

Calamity has been a superordinate element in Yoleño
history since the founding of the pueblo. Centuries of
living in the shadow of impending disaster which they
are powerless to avert have made most Yoleños deferential, skeptical and extremely accommodative before nature
and nature's God.

Onchocerciasis, with its attendant possibility of blindness, is only the most bizarre of a host of catastrophies
which assail the pueblo.

*The fact that this disease has grave manifestations such as
blindness and* mal morado *which cannot fail to impress the
observer leads to the opinion that this is the greatest problem
of the whole region. But in actual fact it is but one of the*

*host of enemies which beset the innumerable Mexican groups
who live in ignorance of their own country, victims of exploitation, poverty, ignorance and ill health.*

[MONTEMAYOR 1954:96]

Poisonous snakes, pneumonia and a host of respiratory
furies, measles, lethal lightning storms, malaria, numerous other acute chronic diseases, whooping cough, floods,
droughts, fires, venomous lizards, earthquakes, hurri-
canes, hunger and a running land feud are all established
expectations and have conditioned the Yoleño to expect
the worst.

This traditional, ongoing body of calamitous precedence
and its resultant ingrained predisposition toward negative anticipation exert a profound influence upon village
character and is the aspect of their history with which
villagers are primarily concerned.

A climate of catastrophy made the Chinantec a wary
conservative. Centuries of submission, grinding poverty
and a high death rate have eliminated optimism as a serious factor in Chinantec personality. Unalloyed optimism
simply does not play any serious part in the thinking of
most villagers. Both experience and custom dictate an
attitude of deferential but profound skepticism toward
altruism, natural benignity and divine love. Divine authority is regarded as the most compelling source of
coercion.

Villagers are assiduously devoted to the detection of
interested motives in human interaction. This pessimistic
evaluation of human motives approaches the fantastic
when villagers are speculating about human behavior
beyond their customary experience. Most villagers were
amused by the speculation of an elderly blind woman

about my reasons for coming to Yolox. She had it on impeccable authority from someone else who was all but infallible in the fathoming of mysteries of this kind that I had come to "strike the people" with my iron cane. After being struck, the people would, in some manner all the more sinister for its indefiniteness, be transported to my *"tierra."*

Persons of all degrees of sympathy and integrity are the vehicles of innovation in the village. And Yoleños are the thrice shy children of oft bitten fathers. A minority of younger villagers, young men who have hired on as *braceros* (laborers) in the tobacco estates of tierra blanca or young women who have taken domestic service in Oaxaca de Juárez or even Mexico City, are zealous proponents of change. A few older men with wider experience characterize their pueblo as *"muy atrazado"* (very backward). An often *pro forma* longing for, as often as not, untasted leeks and melons is an essential ingredient of the conversational stock and trade of the most correct of *"los correctos."*

But the confounding of the faith in progress occasioned by the collapse of just one "all-weather" cardboard house is all but complete. One shopkeeper refused to be a party to this lucrative, if somewhat dubious, project. But at least one other did sell the cardboard slats. It apparently did not occur to anyone of those expressing reservations concerning the imperviousness of the new cardboard to test it. Even if it had occurred to anyone to examine this claim empirically, such an examination would have cost more than 7 pesos, a sum sufficient to sustain many a village family for days. In the end, it was not the cost of the new building material or even the grave reservation about its alleged superiority to that cardboard they had seen before which decided potential customers against it so much as its novelty.

A cautious accommodation also characterizes the relation between the Yoleños and the natural and supernatural worlds. The struggle to "pull bread from among these stones" militates against the emergence of a dominant natural aesthetic. Standing in the midst of the same mountain grandeur which provoked the grudging admiration of even that highly ambivalent commentator on the Mexican scene, Aldous Huxley (1960:195–98), a devoted son of the pueblo did not hesitate to describe his municipio as "very ugly."

Even the perception of those aspects of nature remote from the experience of villagers are tinged with the same quality of menace and foreboding.

I think the sea is a great blue lagoon that goes around the great lands of the earth. It is a very long journey to the place where the sea is to be found. Many bad things could happen to anyone who would go on such a long journey. His beasts might die or the strangers might rob him. Perhaps the strangers would deceive him and not show him the correct path to the sea and even if he reached the land where the sea stays, who can say what the sea would do when he got there.

[J. O. FIELD NOTES]

We are too poor to go to see it [the sea] because it is such a great distance from us, but who can say that it will not choose to come to our pueblo and kill many of us.

[M. B. P. FIELD NOTES]

None of the school-aged children asked to talk about the sea had ever seen it. Yet the note of impending threat which is a part of village thinking about familiar forces of nature was universal in their comments, questions and descriptions of the ocean. Most Yoleños, irrespective of their ages, have had no firsthand experience of the sea but those who can be induced to conjecture about it do so with a kind of deferential diffidence which the community reserves for speculation about natural forces.

There is a marked tendency to reckon time and to remember important events coincidentally with natural disasters or grievous personal misfortune. An old man asked to give his age is very likely to count laboriously from the year in which he lost his sight and combine the years on either side of this crucial year to arrive at an approximation of his present age. February is remembered as the month in which the poisonous snakes begin their journey up the slope to the high pueblo. August is remembered as the month in which "the people have even less to eat."

The most assiduous resignation is demonstrated before natural forces and nature's Patron. The salient attribute of divine character in the prevailing village view is not mercy, love, or even justice but unqualified power. He is quite literally the "Storm King." His rainbow withers the hand of anyone impudent enough to point at it. His eclipse kills the child in the womb. His servant, lightning, strikes at His bidding. His dire retributive wrath is manifest in the rain cloud, the trembling ground and the serpent's mouth. His chief delight is in the doing of His sovereign, unalterable will. Village religiosity is almost exclusively concerned with remaining anonymous before the Lord. The idea of a pious man taking issue with God in the manner of Levi Yitzchak (1816) is even more distasteful than terrestrial face-to-face disputation. Needless to say, the notion of anyone wrestling a blessing from *Tata Dios* or any of His agents struck most villagers as dangerous blasphemy.

The generally held conviction that all but unalterable might is the dominant divine characteristic militates very strongly against a firm belief in the efficacy of even the most meticulously performed reciprocal ritual. The same assiduous avoidance of intensity which is a pronounced feature of most other interaction is evident in ritual practices. "Sometimes the sons of the pueblo will contribute to buy a mass to ask God to spare the maize, but we do not pray in our fields or kill chickens or turkeys there as the Zapotecans do" (M. B. E. Field Notes).

The traditional defense is phlegmatic compliance to the mandate of divine, natural, parental, and communal authority. There is an ingrained communal conviction that much more is required of anyone to whom much is given. The dominant Chinantec personality defense is a sierra variation of the old Army Game, in which eccentricity is tantamount to volunteering.

This cultural inclination to ask little of God, the stranger, and their paisanos, and to expect the worst from all three is probably a prime element in the resistance encountered by medical and paramedical personnel of the Mexican Government's National Campaign against Onchocerciasis.

The Chinantec have devised their own means of meeting all stressful agencies in their calamitous context. These traditional responses to particular stressful agencies are intended not to control or eradicate but to restore a balance, however adverse.

A fool says to himself, I will do this thing or that thing.
I will go here or I will go there. A wise man knows that he
will do the things he is permitted to do and that his going and
coming is not his business. Does the child say now I will cry
for bread? Did we who are blind say that the sight of our
eyes was a burden to us? Who in this world can say what he
will do and where he will go. If one man begins a task, who
will finish it?—if it be finished at all. If you eat mushrooms
or cast beans, will you really discover how your life is to be?
[S. C. S. FIELD NOTES]

Yoleños do not conceive of man as being the measure of all or even most things. There is a customary conviction that anonymity or, failing that, accommodation before God, nature and the powerful stranger is the best that can realistically be expected in this world.

Here we cure ourselves with herbs of the field. There are a few
people in the community who know how to cure this way. I've
tried medicine from the stores but it didn't work very well.
And sometimes I get somebody to burn a candle for me before
one of the images, or I make a vow. And when you don't have
money that's how you live. We are poor here so we drink
our herb tea, burn our candles, make our vows and hope for a
miracle. [P. L. V. FIELD NOTES]

APPENDIX I: FIELD ORIENTATION
AND METHODOLOGY

As the data from which these observations are drawn were amassed without the vital modality of sight, perhaps some detailing of the field orientation and methodology of the observer is in order.

My first knowledge of the existence of San Pedro Yolox was derived from the responses of those persons whose opinions regarding the proposed project had been requested. Dr. Margaret Mead solicited the comments and suggestions of Dr. Julio de la Fuente of the Instituto Nacional Indigenista, Dr. Howard F. Cline, Director of the Hispanic Foundation of the Library of Congress, Dr. Eric Wolf of the Department of Anthropology at the University of Michigan, Dr. John Crawford and Mr. Frank Robbins of the Summer Institute of Linguistics in Mitla, Oaxaca, regarding the implementation of the National Institutes of Health Project "Role of expectation of blindness in a Oaxaca village." A number of Chinantec- and Zapotec-speaking communities of northeastern Oaxaca appeared to satisfy the requirements of the project and it was decided to devote a portion of the Mexican prefield orientation stage to choosing among these possible research sites. I followed the course of these consultations through synopses of the correspondence which were transcribed into braille by Mr. James Yohannan.

My acquaintance with the topography of northeastern Oaxaca was initiated by Mr. Michel Merle's accurate and imaginative translation into relief charts of a large detailed map of that region generously supplied by Dr. Julio de la Fuente.

Mr. Merle and Mr. Yohannan, both extremely knowledgeable photographers, arranged practice sessions to test the feasibility of my attempting field photography. My personal performance at this skill varied from extremely poor to adequate. The variability of my performance did not preclude the probability of my being able to instruct a sighted Spanish-speaking informant in the use of a simple camera or the possibility of finding a villager who had already acquired some skill in photography. Such an instrument was included in my field equipment and both possibilities materialized.

Mr. Cecilio Martinez arranged fourteen transcription sessions totaling approximately thirty-five hours at which he and other Spanish speakers permitted me to perfect the braille shorthand I had devised for recording field data.

Reasonable proficiency with the typewriter has been an approximated goal of mine since fourth grade. A durable portable typewriter and a great quantity of specially treated typing paper requiring no carbon were carried into the field. Notes were typed in triplicate. The municipal secretary, as it transpired, was already skilled in the use of a typewriter, and he extracted for my use selected archival data from the village records, as did two other young men of the village.

Steps were taken to minimize, insofar as possible, the sheer physical difficulties of travel in the broken, rocky, steeply inclined countryside of northeastern Oaxaca. The absence of motor roads in much of this region and the dispersed character which distinguishes its villages made riding an all but indispensable field skill. My initial instruction in riding was with saddle horses on relatively flat ground, but it provided confidence and sufficient competence to make the transition to muleback in the Sierra Juárez.

None of the six conventional collapsible steel canes taken to the field survived the first month of use in that rigorous environment and I had many occasions to be glad of the technical skill of Dr. Dexter Jeannotte who made for my use three extra-length solid steel canes. These canes proved to be excellent probing and supporting implements for negotiating the steep, stepped stony paths of the village and all three of them survived extremely hard use.

The Mexican phase of my field orientation was initiated by a brief but valuable period of consultation in Mexico City, from April 5 to April 12 of 1963, with Dr. Julio de la Fuente and Mr. Salomón Nahmad, the graduate social anthropologist who was my guide and resource person during this initial phase.

The period from April 12 through May 25 was spent in the provincial capital of Oaxaca de Juárez and the adjacent town of Mitla. These forty-two days were devoted to perfecting the Spanish which I had learned through contact with Spanish-speaking Negroes, for the most part Matanceros, in the Cuban barrio of Tampa, Florida. This time was also devoted to an investigation of possible research sites. I made use of data on both Chinantec- and Zapotec-speaking communities in the Oaxaca onchocerciasis zone. This information was secured at the Oaxaca City offices of the National Campaign against Onchocerciasis and consisted largely in a listing of the number of onchocercous blind persons in several villages of that endemic focus. In order to secure more detailed information about possible sites a letter and questionnaire were drafted and circulated among the municipal authorities of the villages with the largest onchocercous blind populations. The letter and questionnaire were disseminated by a Zapotecan courier from Mitla and during personal inspection trips made in the company of a Zapotecan guide. During the course of these investigations a bilingual Yoleño Chinantec, himself the son of a blind man, was encountered and interviewed concerning the onchocercous blind population of his village. His father subsequently became one of my most voluble and knowledgeable informants.

The relative centrality of its settlement pattern, the existence of a Health Center, the small primary character of the village, a high onchocerciasis rate and a large number of onchocercous blind persons all pointed toward San Pedro Yolox as a very suitable research site.

On May 25, 1963, Mr. Nahmad and I traveled by bus to the district seat of Ixtlán where a jeep was hired which conveyed us as close to Yolox as a motorized vehicle could approach. From this point, after several hours of hard walking, we entered the village. My first onchocercous blind informant was encountered laboring up the slope which we were descending. There on the trail, still some hours away from the village, he examined my long steel cane and demonstrated the two sturdy unworked wooden staffs which he used more for support than guidance. That first day on the trail we also met my first child guides and informants who directed us to the village.

We were received hospitably by the village authorities and given to understand that the study would not occasion any negative reaction on the part of the villagers. Preliminary arrangements for my settling in and the securing of mules for the transport of my baggage from the nearest bus stop were initiated.

Having settled upon a site, I returned to Mitla where I parted with Mr. Nahmad, assembled my baggage and set out for Yolox in the company of two Valley Zapotecan guides. Residence was set up in Ixtlán where I received periodic reports via the one telegraph-telephone in Yolox on the state of the dirt road leading to the paths of the village. After a delay of some two weeks, my two guides and I entered Yolox by mule during the first brief hiatus in the heavy summer rains. These guides remained in the village for about three hours after my arrival.

I was initially housed in a small unoccupied dwelling which the village authorities often assigned to guests. As it was located in an isolated portion of the upper part of the village, far from the principal points of interaction, negotiations with one of the largest shopkeepers for the rental of a more centrally located house were begun. A number of villagers had stored belongings in the house I first occupied and the coming and going of villagers, mostly young men, at this point afforded me an opportunity to resolve local curiosity concerning the reasons for my presence in the village and to conduct my first brief interviews.

Most of these brief preliminary interviews were typed. The greater bulk of brailled notes and the consequent difficulty in finding dry storage space for them rendered typing the more practical means of note-taking at that point. The first dwelling I occupied was old and in disrepair. This dilapidation augmented the damage to braille notes occasioned by high humidity and rodents. The house I occupied for the majority of my stay in the village had formerly served a prominent shopkeeper as store and residence. Having improved his situation the merchant had constructed a larger shop and more pretentious residence for his own use and had used the house I rented for storage. My occupancy of this dwelling was delayed pending his relocation of his goods. By mid-July I was domiciled in this sounder, dryer, more centrally situated house and the damage to my notes and equipment was materially reduced. This centrally located house was my residence until the termination of my stay in the village in March of 1964.

The broad general methodological approach formulated prior to my arrival in the village envisaged a progressive familiarity with the Yolox Chinantec emerging from participant observation and the employment of a number of ethnographic interviewing techniques with extensive attention to the onchocercous blind. It was proposed to compensate onchocercous blind informants. Provision was made for the hiring of a bilingual guide and interpreter. Concurrent with this general investigation there was to be a rather more specialized inquiry into the role of the expectation of blindness especially as that negative precedent influences the attitudes and aspirations of villagers.

The implementation of this broad general plan in the actual ethnographic context required constant improvisation. The time of my arrival in the village was especially inappropriate for ethnographic inquiry. Outdoor interaction is at a minimal level during the heavy summer rains. Many householders leave the High Village for the agricultural hamlets. Midsummer is the peak of the period of extreme privation known locally as *"tiempo malo"* (the bad time). Ambiguity concerning the role of the observer was intensified by a number of circumstances. The discourse during my initial reception in the village had served to define generally the reasons for my presence. It was abundantly clear to my hosts that my investigations were unconnected with any of the existing federal hygienic efforts or with any evangelistic campaign. The majority of villagers had not been party to this discourse and hence had no firsthand knowledge as to my purposes. Those Yoleños dispersed on distant downslope parcels received even less direct explanation of my presence and purposes. The prospect of compensation did not attract the onchocercous blind persons whom I knew to be in the village through occasional encounters at points of interaction.

My attempts to clarify my position among that segment of the population where it was most ambiguous—the indigenous monolinguals—were hampered by my lack of fluency in Chinantec and the difficulty of finding a person who could serve both as guide and bilingual interpreter. The offer of the highly placed members of the village Authority to oblige onchocercous blind informants to present themselves for interviews indicated considerable ambiguity as to their own positions regarding my research. My arrival in the village with a social anthropologist who was considered an agent of the State and with letters of recommendation from highly placed personnel of a state agency mounting a local public health effort raised questions concerning the greater Mexican priority of my research. The above-mentioned hygienic effort had encountered general resistance and did employ the local authorities as intermediate figures of suasion. This uncertainty on the part of the local authorities regarding the mandate for my research and the degree of official obligation they were under to assist me was resolved by the character of my role as participant observer, rather than by any formal disavowal of any greater Mexican mandate to compel anyone's cooperation. My reply *"nunca a la fuerza"* (never by force) was not so much grandiloquent as mildly risqué for it carries the additional local meaning that a gentleman never forces his attentions on a lady. This response received wide circulation in the village and because of its brevity was translated with relative fidelity to the more distant settlements.

During my stay in the village, many people requested simple medication. Guided by the previously obtained advice proferred by a Mexican physician, I was generally able to comply with these requests.

It was agreed that one of the *tecticlatls,* or village porters, should serve as interpreter and guide pending my choice of a permanent assistant. As my stay lengthened into weeks, our daily walks and brief interviews and the noting of interaction were mechanical. This first relationship, although courteous, was mutually disadvantageous. The village porter was far more fluent in Chinantec than Spanish. Although he was well compensated it appears that he had not personally sought the assignment but was dispatched by the authorities. So, quite apart from the language barrier, he felt a perceptible and quite understandable lack of interest in the research.

The relationship which developed with my second guide and bilingual interpreter, the son of an onchocercous blind man and a knowledgeable, respected member of his community was quite the reverse. This second interpreter and guide had had lengthy firsthand experience with the onchocercous blind and was fluent both in Chinantec and Spanish. He was a subsistence farmer who was seeking a means of augmenting his income. The temporary character of my first arrangement was generally known and the man mentioned most frequently by persons of differing wealth levels as a possible successor was interviewed. His keen interest in and obvious grasp of the main purposes of the research eminently qualified him for the position which he held intermittently for the duration of the research effort. Even during the brief periods in which the requirements of shifting agriculture called him to attend to his downslope parcels he recommended interested and responsible temporary substitute personnel and his interest in and contributions to the project never lagged. This responsible and intelligent assistant became one of my first primary informants. Through my relationship with him I secured entree to a wide and representative circle of village householders and their families.

My initial dependence upon the prestigious village Authority and my acquisition of a house from the wealthiest man in the village convinced many that my work was not concerned with persons in more marginal circumstances. It transpired that my first guide and bilingual interpreter had supposed it to be part of his responsibility to "see that the señor is not bothered." There was no way of directly refuting this belief. The catholicity of my interest in Yoleños and things Yoleño emerged from my requests for enlightenment concerning the vast inventory of traits of village culture that were new to me. For several days I taped valuable data on village subsistence farming from one of the wealthiest men of the pueblo in the morning and recorded the reflections of one of the most marginal persons of the pueblo in the afternoon.

The first of the onchocercous blind persons who came for a preliminary interview did so more out of regard for my assistant's request that he do so than for the 5-peso remuneration he received. The interview context was informal and festive. Cigarettes and some alcoholic beverage, generally mescal, were always offered. The success of this approach was attested to not only by the quantity of data taken but by the appearance of an elderly onchocercous blind informant whose ambiguity concerning my role had led her to formulate and circulate speculations which had dissuaded other blind persons from participation.

Before mid-September when the breaks in the summer and autumnal rains lengthen and the "bad times begin to soften" the ethnographic context had altered materially. Once established as a person free of any coercive connections with a general desire to "find out how the people live" and who would compensate many of its most marginal inhabitants "just for talking," my problem became one of restricting the number of primary informants.

I planned to relate to the rest of the adult population of the village through an intense ethnographic survey of the onchocercous blind. Once a number of blind persons had assumed the role of primary informant an accurate or at least positive village concept of my role was established.

For all interviews conducted in my house, the same informal festive context was maintained. Interviews were either conducted directly by me in Spanish or through my assistant or other bilingual primary informants in Chinantec. The Matancero cast of spoken Spanish did not occasion any comprehension barrier. It did, however, inspire a short-lived rumor that I was a Cuban espionage agent.

The tape recorder was employed to preserve segments of ordered interaction such as civic festivities, the Independence Day festivities, proceedings during the formal assembly of the village Authority, consultations with members of the village Authority in the presence of other personnel in the municipal hall and formal religious ceremonies. In addition recurrent spontaneous interaction such as childrens' play was also recorded. These segments record the quality of polyphonic discourse in the general contexts of village life. The tape machine was often left in some point of interaction such as a store and segments of varying length were noted.

The machine was also used for the specific preservation of some piece of data contributed by an informant with some specialized knowledge. Thus the village cantor recited the Latin mass in use among the Yolox Chinantec. The village president described the constitution of the village Authority and an onchocercous blind informant came to my house specifically to record his reminiscences of the Mexican revolution of 1910–20. Fixed recording appointments frequently expanded into spontaneous contributions of ethnographic relevance.

Yoleño Spanish is deliberate and tonal, very much like the measured sing-song Spanish of some Scandinavian tourists.

The relative deliberateness of expression reduced the difficulty of recording it via the braille writer or the typewriter. Braille script or braille transcribing devices had never been seen by any informant. Requests for demonstration and the novelty of braille itself and of a blind person using a typewriter decelerated the already leisurely character of the interview context. My regard for accuracy was matched by an effort on the part of most informants to make certain that their data was correctly recorded.

Initially both the extremely free and the very specific interviewing techniques were avoided. Once a number of primary informants had been chosen they were sometimes asked to evaluate questionnaires designed to obtain specific data from secondary informants. Their opinions were in themselves indicative of Yoleño ethos. The choice was often ethnographically revealing.

As key informants came to the realization that they were being asked to describe their culture many people offered skills and knowledge. One villager presented me with a map which he had drawn. He would not accept any direct compensation for his trouble. Books thought to be relevant were loaned to me. Sketches were drawn for me. I was informed well in advance of coming events thought to have relevance to my research.

As data amassed from participant observation combined with insights derived from open-ended interviews to produce a main concept of the general functioning of Yoleño society, it was possible to employ both unstructured and more directed interview techniques.

Questionnaires designed to secure specific data from selected samples of secondary informants relating to mendicancy, charity, concepts of health and illness, income range, compadrazgo, marriage, childrens' contributions to subsistence, microtranshumance and fiesta attendance were personally administered, generally in Spanish and sometimes through a Chinantec interpreter. As most of these questionnaires were administered in the homes of the respondents, the braille board slate was the most practical instrument for noting responses.

The most unstructured approaches were generally employed in securing data from children and the most personal and intimate reflections of adults. The tape recorder, being the least intrusive mechanical aid for this purpose, was most often employed.

In addition to the birth, death, and marriage statistics copied from the municipal archives, assistants were trained to make faithful copies of numerous pertinent documents from the same repositories.

EXCERPTS FROM AN INTERVIEW WITH
A FIFTY-EIGHT-YEAR-OLD BLIND MAN

I didn't become blind suddenly. Darkness did not come all at once. It started little by little by little. It started on the right side. Even though I was blind in my right eye, there was still the left. So I still worked. I always worked. But when the left eye was closed then I became blind. Now I do not work. I am sad because I think of what I could do when I was well. I think about going to work. I think about going to tend my stock, mules, or bulls. I think about going to glean, to clear the bush, to cut coffee, but now I can't. I think about it all the time and that's why I'm sad all the time because now I can't do anything. Now I tell you I can do nothing here. Except to pull weeds when it's time to cultivate the milpa—then I go to pull weeds in the milpa. And down there in my rancho when it's time I can also weed a little coffee, a little cane. But when that's done I can't do anything else.

Observer: Do you know the word philosophy?

No.

Observer: Philosophy means your thoughts about life.

Well I don't think anything about life except to wonder how I am going to get something to eat and how I am going to find a way to clothe myself. I have to content myself from day to day because I think only of how I am going to begin another day. How? If I'm going to eat, where is it going to come from? Where is the money going to come from to buy my clothes? That's what I think about every day. That's why I'm sad all the time. Where is it going to come from? How am I to get corn? How can one get anything like this? That's what I think.

Observer: What is the cause of blindness?

Blindness, what is that?

Observer: You can't see now, right?

No.

Observer: Why?

Why? Who knows why! So I don't know what happened. What I think, what I believe, what I want is that there should be some medicines which would cleanse my eyes. That's what I think all the time. That's what I think about each day. What a pity it is that there is no one who tells me that this, with this you are going to be cleansed, with this you will be able to see. And that's the only thing I think very much about. Because every day, morning and evening, now I think how I'm going to make it. How? If God would give me a miracle so that I could work, so that I could get well so that I could work, so that I could maintain myself, like before, when I could see, when I could see well, when there was nothing at all wrong with me. This is what I think all the time. Oh well, what a pity that I can't find a remedy so that I could see again, so that I could work, so that I could have money so that I could buy a few things, so that I could eat.

A person who swears to a lie before the Ayuntamiento may be fined anywhere from 50 to 60 pesos and more if it's a grave offense. There is a story about a man who cut a bunch of bananas. And then the owner of the bananas came before the Authority and said, "This man has cut my bananas without my permission and they were very good—worth at least 15 pesos, and I request that you make him pay me their value." And the president said, "This is a matter for the *síndico*," and he asked the chief of police to send two policemen to bring the síndico. And the policemen went directly to the thief and brought him to the municipio, and as the owner had seen the offense they put him in the jail, and the next day they brought him before the Ayuntamiento. The síndico said to the policeman, "Please take that man out of jail." And the síndico said to the accused man, "Why were you put in jail?" "I do not know," he said, and then the síndico said to the judicial secretary, "Make a note of that." And they asked him three times why he had been put in jail. Then after the third time the síndico said, "Look here, you are before the Authority of your pueblo and the reason why you were put in prison is well known to all of us and if you will not confess then we shall imprison you yet again in that prison from which there is no escape." And then they handed him grave digging tools. And then the thief was struck with fear and confessed trembling, "señores I know that because of my folly in cutting fruit which was not mine to cut you have most justly put me in this jail, and I ask your pardon and pray you will spare my life." And the síndico said, "We are not here to play with thieves, send him again to the jail from which you took him." And he had to pay a fine of 99 pesos.

The man who payed the 99-peso fine was then obliged to do public works like sweeping the atrium of the municipio so that then any passerby might see him and then ask, "What are you doing?" Then he would say, "I'm doing public works." "And why," the stranger or the child would ask, and then he would have to tell of his misdeed. And the strangers and the children will say either "You deserve your punishment for thus you will learn to leave off evil doing" or they will say, "Ah poor señor, I feel for you but it is through your own misdeeds that you have brought this misfortune upon yourself." My father told me about that case.

PRECEDENCE TALE RECOUNTED BY
A THIRTEEN-YEAR-OLD BOY

They say that there was a *paisano* who did a great deal of wickedness a long long time ago. I don't know all the bad things he did, but he did many, and would not listen to the good advice of anybody—not even the priest. Well, of course they told him to stop doing all the wickedness but he was very bravo and answered all his paisanos and even the priest, and even his father, I think, with very hard words. So this paisano went on like that doing all kinds of bad things until one day he did a thing that was so bad that God got very displeased with him and clouded his eyes for that bad thing he did that day. They say that this paisano became very sad then and was always getting people to burn candles for him, but all those candles, even the very largest ones, did no good and this paisano lived a very long time, but his eyes were never unclouded.

PRECEDENCE TALE RECOUNTED BY
AN ELEVEN-YEAR-OLD GIRL

They say that there was a woman of Temextitlán that never wanted to agree with anyone. She was going to sell a chicken and she met a stranger and she said many bad things to this stranger and lied to him and deceived him about a path and the stranger fell in the river and he got very sick. Then this woman from Temextitlán that lied to the stranger met a paisano one day who was blind. He wanted her to give a little charity but she would not. I think she had many chickens and even many turkeys but she would not give anything and she was rude to that paisano that was blind who asked for the charity. So God noticed that and decided to close her eyes forever. So He did that and would not hear any of her prayers.

DREAM OF A TWELVE-YEAR-OLD BOY

I thought about the sea and how it might look and I dreamed about the sea. In my dream of the sea I went on a long journey on the water and there were some paisanos in a country which I saw in the sea and they said I should go back and bring all the people to the country that I found in the sea. And when I was coming to tell the Authority about this fine flat country, my eyes were clouded so that I could not find the pueblo or go back to the sea pueblo.

COMMENTS AND DREAM OF A TEN-YEAR-OLD GIRL

I must tell you that those boys were wrong. Girls do know how to play marbles, some of them do. But when they get a little older they don't play marbles. . . . My father says that your tierra is very far away and that there are many people there. Don't you miss your tierra sometimes? Doña A—— is afraid of your iron stick. She thinks you will strike the people with it. My father said she should not say such things. I think that it is a beautiful stick and that it makes a lovely sound when it rings on the stones. . . . Our poor paisanos whose eyes have been closed have been given very bad luck. It is a very sad thing to think about that—sometimes I have to cry for them. That is how it is, some people get sad lives and other people get happy lives. . . . I do like to go to school, but sometimes I dream that a bad thing happened to P—— or me at school. Once I had a dream that R—— and I found a civics book and I took it from her and ran away, but then I could not read the civics book because my eyes were closed.

COMMENT OF AN ELEVEN-YEAR-OLD BOY

Sometimes thinking about how it would be with me if my eyes were clouded makes me very sad. You have a finger-writing machine and a finger watch and you give many little fiestas, but would it not be much better for you if your eyes were not clouded? I think it is better to live with clear eyes than to have many fine things.

Drawings of local house types as executed by an adult primary informant.

EXCERPTS FROM PERSONAL FIELD OBSERVATIONS

S—— V——, blind in left eye because of
onchocerciasis September 23, 1963

While I was interviewing him, L—— came up very disturbed
and said "No." And I said "Why no?" "Because he can see"
was the reply. And then G—— came in and he was very upset
too and he said, in his English. "This one he have of the eyes—
one, this one he have much of the money and you should not
give him nothing—nothing for him." It seems that because he
has the sight of one eye the Yoleños do not consider him to be
blind. Later on, several of my paisanos, or so they described
themselves. came by to tell me that I had been hoodwinked
because "that V—— fellow" has a lot of money and I should
not have given him the 5 pesos which I gave him. Doña J——
took the payment of the 5 pesos as being an extreme indication
of my profligacy and her father, Don M—— offered his assistance in grabbing the scoundrel by his pants' leg and shaking
out the 5 pesos. G——, her husband, offered to thrash the fellow for me and to recover the 5 pesos. L—— expressed the
opinion that it was all his fault because he should have been
there to make sure that *mala gente* (bad people) of that odious
stripe were barred from my door. I made an attempt to explain
that there are at least as many mala gente as *buena gente*
(good people) in any pueblo and if I were to know Yolox I had
to get to know its thieves and villains as well as people like
themselves. L—— took this remark very kindly and began to
chuckle but the net result of this whole indoctrination was very
negative for, at the end of this peroration when I asked him if
he understood what I said, he said, "Si, don Juan, but you
should not let mala gente come into your house."

The W—— affair, December 16, 1963

The president told me today that a German gentleman came to
Yolox, R—— W——, speaking of an improved municipio with

two floors. He was linked with the Italian construction company which was, or so they said, interested in building a road to Yolox. He, W——, said he wanted to take the document, "titulo y mapa con explicación del mapa" to Mexico. He did, and after written entreaty for its return, the pueblo dispatched Miguel to Mexico City. He was ignored by W——, but finally elicited the information that he, W——, had handed the document over to some of the officials of the Italian company: P——, R——, S——, and two others whom I cannot remember. One of them lives in Sicily. They said their families wanted to see the documents. They were not insured and no kind of guarantee was given for their safe return.

I advised with cautious reservation that they write concerning the matter to the President of the Italian Republic and to the Secretary of State of the Vatican. And there the matter rests I think.

SELECTED RESPONSES TO QUESTIONS
ONE, TWO, EIGHT, NINE AND TEN
OF A TEN-QUESTION SCHEDULE
DESIGNED TO ELICIT DATA ON
CONCEPTS OF HEALTH
AND ILLNESS

Question 1. Do you have much illness?

Not now. I don't know why, I go to the rancho like everyone else but I haven't had a single nodule taken out. It might be because I bathe every day while I'm there and put alcohol on myself. The Authority is always telling people to bathe every day that they're there and to put alcohol on afterward. My wife and I do that and nothing has ever happened to us.

No. My son has had a pain in his whole body for about five years. I think it is contagious, and I got it from him. I have pain in my arms and legs and I am losing my sight. Have you a medicine that will help us?

Not much, only my wife, she's not very strong. I think it's being tired from her work, hard work in the fields, we're not generally sick—of course, there is that son of mine who died last year.

My wife has headaches which interfere with her hearing. I have toothaches. Nothing else.

Onchocerciasis no, but susto yes. The Comaltepecos gave my wife *espanta* (sudden fright), and my wife and all the children have had illness as a result of susto the Comaltepecos caused. She confronted them and told them they were cowards for coming when they knew all the men were away. They threw three bombs in the house and since then they've all been sick.

We have some because of aires. My wife does also.

I think so.

My father and my mother aren't well because of aire.

Not much illness, they just died.

My wife had to go to Mexico for an operation. We have cough, grippe and my eldest son has bronchitis. We took him to Oaxaca and Mexico.

My brother-in-law is sick. He has the sickness which makes you fall on the floor. My head aches and my whole body also.

Question 2. What remedies do you use?

Leaves of aire for heart pains. We make a tea of them. We use tea leaves for colds.

Before we had many remedies, but now we can buy them in the stores. We use coffee and mescal for upset stomachs, herb tea for colds. Cuts we wash with leaves of aire.

Mejoral (patent medicine).

We use mejoral from the stores, but in the house we use water —we sit them in hot water.

My wife is getting injections at the Health Center.

Here we cure ourselves with herbs of the field. There are a few people in the community who know how to cure in this way. I've tried medicine from the stores but it didn't work very well. And sometimes I get somebody to burn a candle for me before one of the images, or I make a vow. And when you don't have money that's how you live. We are poor here so we drink our herb tea, burn our candles, make our vows and hope for a miracle. The illness I have, that's important to me. They say there isn't any remedy for it and that I have to go to Oaxaca or Mexico to get a bottle of medicine that would cure me of this.

If I fall seriously ill I don't try to cure myself, but seek the help of a *curandero* (local herbalist).

For the most part we use herbs. Once in a while we buy medicine from the store, but we're mostly in the rancho and it's nothing but herbs.

Ammonia water—we massage with it. I use medicine water for my leg.

Mejoral or a cup of bitter coffee.

We don't know anything about remedies.

For susto we take baths with herb tea and blow *tepache* (cane juice) fumes over the body. We hold the liquor in the mouth and then blow it over the entire body three times a day. The patient stands with his clothes on and the curandero holds liquor in his mouth and blows it all over the patient, then the patient lies down. He doesn't get really wet, just a little moist.

We sometimes buy medicine, but generally we use herbs mostly mixed with aguardiente and mescal. It's good for the children too.

Bitter coffee with leaves of aire. We burn tobacco leaves and massage the area that has aire with ashes.

We sit in hot water.

For a bad cold we take hot cinnamon tea with a little mescal with sugar and lemon juice. Aguardiente is stronger. Sometimes we put our feet in hot water with alcohol. We boil leaves of aire for a cold. There are two kinds of tea made with the leaves of chamiso. When tired after work they relax the veins and blood. One is for the veins, the other is for the blood. We boil them and drink them.

We use herbs, but mostly they just calm, they don't cure.

I use lime water, I don't want to take pills because I went to the Health Center and took some pills and came back and lay down and then got sick.

We use injections, pills, spoonfuls of this or that.

Question 8. How many blind people are there in Yolox?

Nine.

Who knows? Maybe eight. Two died last year.

Oh there are a lot—fifty or sixty.

I don't know.

About six or seven.

About ten.

Eighteen.

Four.

An awful lot—about eleven or twelve.

There are sixteen in Yolox.

I don't know. I only know one—P——.

Question 9. Are there more blind people in Yolox than elsewhere?

Yes, because the population is bigger.

No, because other pueblos are larger and therefore have more.

Yes I think so.

Who knows? Possibly there are more in Totomoxtla which is an agencia of Quiotepec.

Seems like more here. The municipio has four agencias and they have blind people too.

I don't know.

There are more here than in other pueblos. I don't know why, there are more people—maybe other places are just little pueblos. From time to time a few come from here and a few come from other pueblos. One of these poor people died in my house.

This is a small pueblo so there are few here. In large pueblos there are more.

Seems like there are more here, but no one has told me.

There are fewer here than in other places.

Possibly, it depends on the pueblo. For example, Comaltepec is larger, possibly there are more there than here.

I think so, it's hard to tell. People tell me about blind people I've never seen and people tell me that they're blind, but I don't know.

I think it's about the same everywhere.

I don't know really since I just came here a few years ago and no one has told me.

Of course. There are many here.

Yes, I have seen many.

There are more in Totomoxtla. I think there are about five there.

Question 10. What causes the blindness?

God. Who knows? Onchocerciasis.

Onchocerciasis.

Some people blame the operation and others blame another thing and some don't have the operation, but I don't know.

Why? People are careless. If they get wet in the fields they don't do anything about it.

I don't know.

When we come into this world our luck goes before us and if it has been decided that we will be blind, we will be.

I don't know very well how this illness is born, but you understand, we're poor people and we have to work in the fields and sun strikes us all day and when the sun stops the rain strikes us and we go loaded with our burdens when we leave the fields and before the road came near we had to carry even more and our land is very ugly, nothing but mountains and bush and I think that's why the blindness strikes us, but I'm not sure.

Some are blind from onchocerciasis, others from cataracts.

I don't know about the women, but a lot of times it comes from men quarreling and hitting each other in the eyes with stones.

When people come up from the rancho or from working in the fields they are sweating or sometimes it is raining and their clothes dry on them.

It depends on where they go—when they go to places, their ranchos, where it is hot they get their clothes wet. When they come up from the hot wet, down country they are sweating and take off their shirts and permit the air to enter the pores of their sight and their whole body but you understand that down there it's hot and wet and on the way up they pass through hot dry country and this is a drastic change and this change causes the blindness. You will note that people who go from here to Carrizal where it's hot and dry never go blind.

Onchocerciasis, so they say.

Humidity, rains, and flies which bite them.

They work hard, carrying heavy things. They open their shirts, their pores open and then they come back up here and cold fresh air hits them and penetrates their pores and cools their blood. I don't know exactly, but people tell me it's the hot wet climate. I don't know, but I think that's why. Who knows?

They live in the hot down lands and then come walking up in the hot sun, then they take their clothes off and bathe in the cool rivers, that's it.
Onchocerciasis, aire, sometimes because they leave for other pueblos.

I think it has to do with el aire.

Who knows? Depends on animals, water—who knows? So many reasons.

Because we have low-lying ranchos and animals which bite people and other pueblos do not.

The luck of each one.

ACCOUNT OF THE EVENTS
TRANSPIRING THE SIXTEENTH AND
SEVENTEENTH OF FEBRUARY 1962
AS STATED BY AN EYEWITNESS

I, Manuel S. Santiago, coming from the city of Oaxaca on the sixteenth of February, 1962, coming from the *vereda* (main trail), saw two men hidden, those who are thought to have come to assault [us on] the third day, or February 17, our neighbors from Santiago Comaltepec. They mounted an assault against the population of the community of San Pedro Yolox. Finding ourselves with 20 men to defend the pueblo, seeing [by their] bloody deeds that those neighbors wanted to wipe the people of Yolox off the map, being about seven in the morning, the firing broke out around the community of Yolox. Finding ourselves exposed, in all, six men ascended to the *campanario* (belfry), eight [went to] the rectory, four men went to the corridor of the municipio and two fled to the *rancherías* to tell the rest of the men of the pueblo that Yolox was the victim of assassins from Comaltepec. The firing lasted seven hours. Meanwhile the federal authorities received a call for help [and news] of the aggression we were suffering. In the evening when help arrived, we gave an account of the deaths we had suffered, being the following: Maria Ruíz Flores, Celerina Rivera, Joel García, Carlos Gutierrez.

DEATH CERTIFICATE OF MARIA RUIZ FLORES

In the pueblo of San Pedro Yolox, district of Ixtlán de Juárez, state of Oaxaca, being seven 7 o'clock on the seventeenth 17 of the month of February of nineteen hundred and sixty-two.

Señor Emilio Flores, thirty years of age, appeared before the undersigned municipal president announcing the death of his wife, Maria R. F., a woman of Mexican nationality, a native of this place, twenty-two 22 years of age of 4 Calle Benito Juárez, as a consequence of wounds inflicted by firearms. Her parents, Pedro Ruíz and Concepción Flores, being campesinos, residing at the aforementioned address, declared the deceased to be of the age noted. The Coroner's Office* being closed, this act was duly noted before the following witnesses, Mario Vargas and Tomás Arias, native born citizens of this pueblo, campesinos of legal age and unrelated to the party in whose interest this

---

* In actual fact there is no Coroner's Office in Yolox, and the formal recording of deaths appears to be rare. The meticulous registering of this death and at least one other was probably occasioned by the unusual nature of the deaths and by the hope that they might serve as evidence in any federal inquiry and in obtaining redress in the Yoleño case against the Comaltepecos.

certificate has been drawn in conformity with the burial statute. Enacted this day, read and attested to by the witnesses who have here affixed their names with the municipal president.

Certified by the Municipal President

signed/*Hermán Flores Martinez*

WITNESSES. signed/*Mario Vargas Santiago*
signed/*Tomás Arias Roja*

TESTIFIER. Emilio Flores Ruíz

SECRETARY. signed/*Antonio Santiago Sánchez*

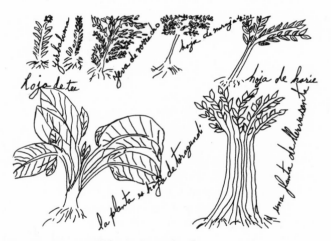

Some important medicinal plants in the Yoleño folk pharmacopoeia drawn by an adult primary informant.

LAST WILL AND TESTAMENT OF
BALTAZAR RODRIGUES

In the pueblo of San Pedro Yolox in the district of Ixtlán in the state of Oaxaca, at ten o'clock on the evening of April 6, 1951.

I, Baltazar Rodrigues, native of this pueblo, finding myself gravely ill and fearing that I will lose the power of speech in my final hour, have had the strength to call upon Señor Juan Salas M. to record my wishes concerning the distribution of the few goods I possess under the following stipulations.

First. It is my wish that the lady, Margarita Gallegos, with whom I have lived and with whom I have had a daughter, my only child, shall remain in my house. If God permits that child to grow up she is to be the legitimate owner of my house, and as for her mother, no one is to dispossess her as long as she wishes to remain there.

Second. If by some misfortune my daughter should die prematurely, responsibility for the house will revert to my cousin, Miguel Rodrigues Santos. As for the sum of $400.00 (four hundred) pesos, $100.00 (one hundred) pesos are to go to my señora, Margarita, and the other $300.00 (three hundred) pesos are to be devoted to the welfare of the church.

Third. I have five pieces of land here in the pueblo known by their Chinantec names as follows: (1) MII QUIA ZIUU, (2) COO TOO HAAN, (3) COO GUÂ, (4) JUU MOO MIU, (5) QUIÁ CUO FUIHI. The undersigned have been empowered by me to fix the limits of each parcel. I bequeath the first four parcels to my cousin, Miguel Rodrigues Santos and the last I leave to my niece, Amalia Reyes.

Fourth. I bequeath my parcels in Rancho Esperanza to my señora, Margarita. There is one on which our jacal is located, the second is a coffee plot where my parents live, the third is a parcel sown partially in coffee and partially in cane, the fourth is a newly cleared plot below Chirimolla near the Río Grande and the fifth is a plot which Señor Marciano Jimenez sold me for the sum of $10.00 (ten) pesos which is located in the same Rancho Esperanza and which I have planted with coffee. These pieces of land, their limits are defined by documents, will maintain my señora for the remainder of her life. After her death they should be sold for the good of the church. I wish to make it clear that some years ago I.gave my niece,

Amalia Reyes, some coffee trees, therefore, no one has to fight over my goods.

Fifth. Two cows now being tended for me by Señor Julio Gallegos, worth $50.00 (fifty) pesos, are both to become the property of my señora, Margarita. Also, a yoke of oxen which I am tending for Señor Esteban Santos, with a value of $30.00 (thirty) pesos, each one of them is. to remain in the care of the same lady until, by mutual agreement, the team is disposed of in accordance with the custom of our pueblo.

Sixth and last wish. Finally I request that Señor Juan Salas, who has heard and recorded the disposition I have made of my goods declare publicly that this is my last will and testament.

Given by Baltazar Rodrigues, who is now unable to sign.

Signed/*Juan Salas Mendoza*

WITNESSES

signed/*Alfonzo Jimenez*   signed/*Celia Salas*

APPENDIX III: THE EPIDEMIOLOGY

OF ONCHOCERCIASIS

One of the most spectacular elements of the general stressful environment of San Pedro Yolox is the flyborne, filarial infection known variously an *onchocercosis,* onchocerciasis, river blindness, or Robles' disease. Although it is not a mortal disease, onchocerciasis is of such grave economic, social and psychological import that its control and eradication is officially viewed as one of the paramount objectives of Mexican public health authorities.

The disease has both an Old World and Western Hemisphere infection gradient. The infected human population of these two foci of endemicity is conservatively estimated at twenty million. The Old World zone of prevalence is a relatively continuous strip extending from West Africa across the west central, central, and east central portions of that continent and beyond to southwestern Arabia. The western terminous of this zone appears to be Dahomey, and its eastern extremity is currently the Yemen. The northern Sudan is the most northerly focus of infection, and centers of infection have been discovered as far south as mainland Tanzania (World Health Organization 1962:421).

The New World onchocerciasis gradient is a narrow belt of infection extending discontinuously from southeastern Mexico through Central America to the northwestern shoulder of the South American mainland. The northwestern terminous of this broken gradient traverses the southeastern Mexican states of Oaxaca and Chiapas. San Pedro Yolox is located in northeastern Oaxaca on the northwestern extremity of this New World endemic zone.

The infectious agent in human onchocerciasis is the filarial worm *onchocerca volvulus*. The areas of endemicity correspond closely with the distribution of certain simulids which are generally thought to be the intermediate hosts. Females of a number of stream-breeding, day-biting, bloodsucking, anthropophylic black flies of the genus *simulium* are the intermediate hosts of the pathogenic agent (Chávez Núñez 1963:21). *S. damnosum* and *S. neavei* are the most instrumental African vectors (Alvarez Amézquita 1962:910) while *S. ochraceum, S. metallicum* and *S. callidum* appear to be the principal New World intermediate hosts (Vargas 1962:960). The *O. volvulus* larvae are ingested by feeding simulids. These microfilariae develop for six or seven days in the thoracic muscles of the fly and are subsequently injected into a permanent human host.

The dominant clinical manifestation of onchocerciasis infection is the formation of tough, fibrous cysts, or nodules, in which the mature filariae are encapsulated. These cysts are most often found on the lower limbs and pelvic girdle in the African form of the disease, but are commonly located on the upper trunk and head in American human onchocerciasis. The progeny of these filariae, however, escape from the cysts to optical and conjunctive tissue. If the incursion of free microfilariae is sustained, the classic, negative optical and dermal alterations associated with the onchocercous syndrome ensue. Progressive lodging of the microfilariae of *onchocerca volvulus* in the optic humors, the cornea, the iris, and the sheath of the optic nerve may lead to acute visual impairment and even total blindness (Torroella 1962:1039–45).

In addition to the negative ocular symptoms of this disease, onchocerciasis also gives rise to a number of dermal alterations. These skin lesions are more numerous in the New World form

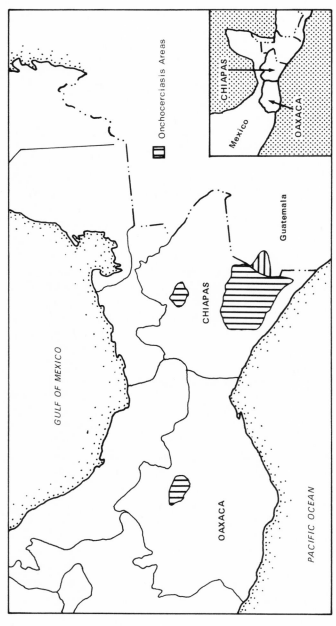

4. Onchocerciasis areas in Mexico and Guatemala

(Based on Mexican Public Health data published in "Epidemiologia de la oncocercosis en México," 1962, Vol. 4, p. 941.)

of onchocerciasis. Of special interest among these dermal lesions is the New World manifestation known as *mal morado crónico* (the purple, or painted, sickness) which imparts a reddish-purple cast to the affected skin. Still another of these skin lesions imparts the appearance of advanced or extreme age (Chávez Núñez 1963:20; Salazar Mallén 1962:1071–74).

Endemic onchocerciasis is confined to noncontiguous portions of two states in the South Pacific region of the Mexican Union. Two of these areas of hyperendemicity, the focuses of Zoconusco and Chamula, are in Chiapas. San Pedro Yolox is in the heart of the third area of high onchocerciasis infection in northeastern Oaxaca. (See Map 4)

The most southerly of these infected regions, the Zoconusco focus, is a 6,800 square kilometer extension of the western Guatemalan focus of Huehuetenango. Mexican public health statistics place the number of infected persons at 30,000 out of a total population for the entire Zoconusco focus of 93,000. The over-all infection rate is estimated at 32.2 percent, but the range of endemicity varies widely within the several subdivisions of the zone.

The second, or central zone of high endemicity is the north Chiapanecan focus, a 700 square kilometer tract of the Sierra Zontehuitz. This region is often referred to as La Zona Chamula because the numerically dominant group in its population is the Tzotzil, popularly called *Chamula*. Of an estimated total focal population of 22,500, some 4,000 are said to be infected, giving a general focal infection rate of 18.2 percent. The same intrafocal variation in infection rates which characterizes the Zoconusco focus obtains in the Tzotzil focus.

The most northerly of these zones of hyperendemicity is the Oaxaca focus. This 1,400 square kilometer area consists of the head waters of the Papaloapan and most of the high broken spur of the Sierra Madre Oriental, called the Sierra Juárez. The endemic focus has a population of 45,000. Some 5,800 persons, or 12.6 percent of the total zonal population, are estimated to be infected. Subdivisions of the Oaxaca focus have widely varying infection rates. Subregions where particularly

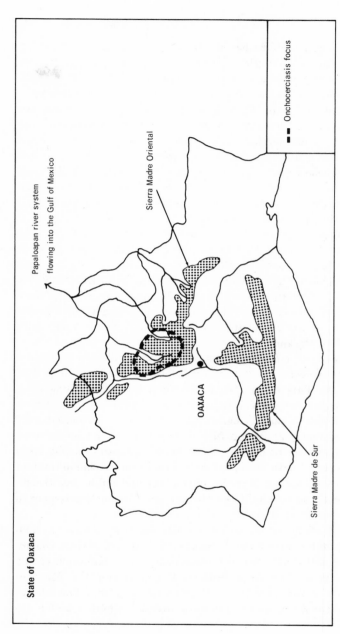

State of Oaxaca

Papaloapan river system
flowing into the Gulf of Mexico

Sierra Madre Oriental

OAXACA

Sierra Madre de Sur

■ Onchocerciasis focus

5. Oaxaca Onchocerciasis focus

(According to Mexican Public Health data published in "Epidemiologia de la oncocercosis en México, 1962, Vol. 4, p. 947.)

favorable ecological conditions for simulid development obtain, such as the hot humid hamlets of San Pedro Yolox, have some of the highest infection rates for the entire Republic. Map 5 illustrates the topographical character of this Oaxaca zone.

There is still disagreement among authorities concerning the origins of the Zoconusco focus. Some maintain that it is an independent, indigenous Chiapanecan area of infection while others tend toward the belief that onchocerciasis spread to this region from adjacent areas of hyperendemicity in Guatemala. The central, or Chamula, focus is said to be of fairly recent origin, dating from the third decade of the present century. The infection is thought to have been carried to this part of northern Chiapas by Tzotzil braceros returning from contract labor on the coffee estates of the Zoconusco focus (García Sánchez and Chávez Núñez 1962:939–58).

The Head of the National Campaign against Onchocerciasis subscribes to the premise that the Oaxaca focus is of African origin. Infected West African slaves landed at coastal points in Veracruz are said to have constituted the first Mexican onchocerciasis reservoir (Chávez Núñez 1963:17–18).

The Mexican public health agency officially charged with the control and eventual eradication of onchocerciasis, the National Campaign against Onchocerciasis, employs the same program of treatment and prophylaxis in all three infected zones.

The publication (Calderón 1917) of the Guatemalan Dr. Rudolfo Robles' findings which details the connection between *O. volvulus* and the characteristic skin lesions and ocular damage associated with onchocerciasis occasioned extensive interest and research among Mexican physicians and public health officials about the possibility of the existence of onchocerciasis in contiguous areas of Mexico.

In 1929 onchocerciasis was officially declared to be a national health problem and a year later the "Campaign against Onchocerciasis and Pinto" was established under the direction of Dr. M. E. Bustamante as a permanent adjunct of the Mexican Bureau of Public Health (Ortiz Mariotte 1963:8). The laboratory and field phases of this effort are coordinated under national supervision from the national antionchocerciasis center at Huixtla, Chiapas.

The standard antifilarial agent employed by the National Campaign against Onchocerciasis since 1948 is a diethylcarbamazine compound known commercially as Hetrasan. Hetrasan is more effective against the larval parasites than the adult filariae. This drug, however, frequently gives rise to severe side effects which occasion massive resistance to its use on the part of the affected population. Suramin, or Moranyl, is also an effective filaricide. This second standard drug is far less frequently employed, however, because the intense therapeutic shock occasioned by Suramin precludes its use under field conditions (Mazzotti 1962:1047–54).

Perspiration minimizes the effectiveness of insect repellents, but some insecticides (notably DDT) appear effective in the later aquatic stages of simulid development (Chávez Núñez 1963:26, 27).

Since 1948 standard field treatment has consisted in administration of Hetrasan and surgical excision of the nodules containing the adult filariae. As yet there is no cure for onchocerciasis and the arrest of the disease is dependent upon sustained use of Hetrasan tablets and repeated excision of the recurrent nodules.

Local authorities in the communities of infected zones are under official obligation to induce the people of their localities to participate in the program of diagnosis and treatment. Paramedical teams are charged with carrying the hygienic effort to the even more remote dependent localities. Eighteen Health Centers in the three zones are serviced by mobile brigades of personnel trained in the national antionchocerciasis center at Huixtla. Physicians visit these field infirmaries to conduct comprehensive diagnosis and administer mass treatment. In addition to the brigades composed of male nurses, the Campaign calls for the permanent residence in the eighteen field infirmaries of female graduates of the two-month course·in the origin, transmission, and arrest of onchocerciasis conducted at the Huixtla Center.

In addition to their diversified paramedical role, graduates of this Huixtla course are charged with the implementation of the broader social and economic aims of the Campaign against Onchocerciasis. Modern greater Mexican standards of hygiene, child care, home economics, and nutrition are interpreted and promoted through the medium of the Health Center and its nurse in permanent residence.

The degenerative ocular manifestations of onchocerciasis increase with age. Findings of the Campaign against Onchocerciasis in 1961 (García Sánchez and Chávez Núñez 1962:950–54) reveal that, of 1,399 infected persons examined in the Oaxaca zone, 31 were totally blind. Only one of the totally blind was below the age of thirty. In a random sample of 9,889 persons, taken in the same year from both Chiapas zones, more than 60 percent of the 4,940 persons found to be infected were above the age of twenty.

Susceptibility does not appear to be materially influenced by race. Caucasoids, Amerindians and persons of both Amerindian and European genetic heritage appear to be equally affected (Chávez Núñez 1963:21, 22).

Given the absence of predisposing genetic factors, it is obvious that economic and cultural factors loom large in the distribution and persistence of onchocerciasis. The steeply inclined, well-watered, heavily forested temperate to semitropical shelf—that vital swath of escarpment lying between 500 and 1,500 meters above sea level—is at once the prime area of human subsistence activity and the optimum area of vector ecology (Ochoterena 1948:277–85).

The number of totally blind persons in any community of an onchocerciasis infected zone is only a partial indicator of the extent to which this disease impinges upon the lives of its inhabitants. The incidence of economic blindness is officially estimated to be twice that for total loss of sight in the Oaxaca zone (Chávez Núñez 1963:24). Quite apart from the grave burden it imposes upon an already extremely marginal population, onchocerciasis retards the exploitation of whole regions of southeastern Mexico.

APPENDIX IV: SURVEY OF THE LITERATURE

PERTAINING TO THE CHINANTEC

The Chinantec-speaking peoples, the Hu-me, the Wah-mi, the Dza-mi, and the Usila group have been the subject of relatively scanty and desultory research. The peripheral status of the Chinantla, their traditional area of provenience, in contrast to larger southern highlands cultures is reflected in the occasional and ancillary literature. The earliest Spanish reference to the Chinantec appears to be Bernal Diāz del Castillo's favorable impression of their martial prowess. But the soldier chronicler's allusion is general and does not distinguish between the several groups of Chinantec-speaking tribes (Díaz del Castillo 1965: 274, 292).

The major elements of the bibliographical corpus from which ethnohistorical reconstructions and other scholarly speculations are derived consist of two late sixteenth-century *relaciones,* or general descriptive reports submitted in response to Philip II's inquiry into the geography, resources and demography of the regions of New Spain (Quijada 1579; Esquivel 1579); two manuscripts, a *visita,* or survey report, dated 1599, and a civil congregation log, or account of the forced removal and resettlement of the population of San Pedro Yolox in 1603 (Ribera 1599; Quiroz 1603); some entries in the late nineteenth-century compendium of descriptive material amassed on Oaxacan communities under Republican auspices (Mechling 1912: 678–81; Gracida 1883:n.p.) ; and Mariano Espinosa's (1961) early twentieth-century general historical survey work.

A survey of the literature (Cline 1956:635–56) cites a number of supplementary cartographic sources which, it is believed, will yield important archeological, geographical and ethnographic data. Specific reference is made to two *lienzos*, or pictographic fabric maps and to various pueblo land maps collected by R. J. Weitlaner (Cline 1961:64–67; 1957:295).

The extremely speculative and hypothetical character of the earliest stages of the ethnohistorical reconstruction of the region is reflected in the title of one of the few scholarly efforts in this direction, *Una subdivisión tentativa de los Chinantecos históricos* [A Tentative Subdivision of the Historic Chinantecs] (Cline 1952–53). Cline (1961:159, 160), commenting on Mariano Espinosa's early chronology for the Chinantla, describes the earliest dates, those from A.D. 1110 to A.D. 1420 as "more or less mythical," those from 1420 to 1527 are considered "possibly traditional," and those from 1527 are referred to as "possibly historical." Rosendo Pérez García (1956[I]:95) describes the Chinantec as being masters of the Chinantla by the early twelfth century of the common era c. 1110.

For about a century after its establishment, the Chinantla appears to have been a single administrative area from c. 1110 to c. 1240, but this initial period of unity was followed by periodic hostility between the highland Chinantec inhabiting the Chinantla Pichinche and the lowland Chinantec-speaking groups of the Chinantla Grande. The civil strife culminated in the definitive division of the Chinantla into two subareas. The administrative center of the lower or Chinantla Grande, was at the town of Chinantla. This region was later subdivided and the extreme southeast of the lower Chinantla was governed independently.

Concurrent with this process of bifurcation which established two subareas in the Chinantla Grande, there was a similar period of fission in the highland, or Chinantla Pichinche. Yoloxeniquila, or Yoloxochitlán, was initially the seat of the entire northwestern or Chinantla Pichinche. By c. 1420, however, immigrants from Yoloxeniquila appear to have established a second center. These two communities, Yoloxeniquila and its similarly named daughter city were known collectively as *los Yolos*, the two Yoloxes, and constituted one of the two highland subdivisions of the northwestern Chinantla. A second Pichinche center, or "kingdom," * formed further north around Usila.

There appears to have been intermittent strife among Chinantec communities within the Chinantla and between the several Chinantec areas and their environing Mazatec, Zapotec, Cuicatec and Mixtec neighbors (Cline 1955:116–17; Espinosa 1961:72–93).

The increasing influence of Central Valley authority is reflected in periodic military incursions in the middle and late fifteenth century. In 1454 the Zapotecans are traditionally supposed to have returned Temasolapan, a highland Chinantec-speaking area, to the jurisdiction of the upland Chinantla to induce the highland Chinantec to form an alliance against the Mexicans (Aztecs). Montezuma I is traditionally thought to have mounted two expeditions in this part of the southern highlands. The first imperial campaign, c. 1454, reduced a portion of the lower Chinantla while a second more ambitious campaign three years later established general Aztecan dominance in much of the Chinantla (Gay 1933[I]:140; Bancroft 1874 [V]:416; Espinosa 1961:122, 123).

The Mexicans are said to have garrisoned the region from Tuxtepec and to have mounted a general campaign in the region under Montezuma II shortly before the arrival of the Spaniards (Cline 1957:274; Iturribarria 1955:54; Pérez García 1956[I]:61–63).

The highland Chinantecan and Zapotecan pueblos of what is now the Sierra Juárez were finally reduced by Martín de la Mesquita in 1527, six years after the capitulation of Tenochtitlán (Cline 1955:117; Pérez García 1956[I]:75).

---

* Kingdom is a translation of the Spanish term *reinado*, often used to refer to these precontact Chinantec subdivisions. There is nothing to indicate that they were in actual fact monarchical entities.

The region of the northern Sierra Juárez environing Yolo-xeniquila, or los Yolos, and the Zapotecan pueblo of Maquiltian-guis was the spoil of the Rodriguez de Salas family for at least three generations. Juan Rodriguez de Salas, the first *encomen-dero* (fief holder), acceded to his fief in 1527 and it remained the feudal legacy of his heirs long after the forced removal and resettlement of the population of old Yoloxeniquila, or los Yolos, in 1603 (Cline 1955:118).

Civil congregation, or forced removal and resettlement, had been an ongoing aspect of colonial policy in New Spain since its inception. The application of this general aspect of Spanish colonial policy in the specific instance of the Rodriguez de Salas *encomienda* (land grant) of Yoloxeniquila and Maquiltianguis required some four years.

The population of Yoloxeniquila, or los Yolos, was obliged to quit their traditional site and resettle in a new one chosen by a survey team acting under vice regal mandate. The *visita*, or recommendations of the Ribera vice regal survey team, suggested the resettlement of the population of old Yoloxeniquila and its subject hamlets at the present site (Ribera 1599).

The resettlement, or congregation, is described in the *Historia del pueblo de Yolox en su congregación en el año de 1603* (Archivo General de San Pedro Yolox 1884) and is said to parallel closely the official journal kept by Captain Alonzo de Quiroz, the official charged originally with the responsibility for the resettlement (Cline 1955:128–29).

Along with the mechanics of military management, one of the dominant motives for the forced removal and resettlement of Indian groups was the facilitation of their conversion. The mission to the Chinantec was most intensive and organized among the groups inhabiting the lower, or Chinantla Grande. This portion of the region was crown land and its conversion the responsibility of the Dominican order. That portion of the Chinantla around San Pedro Yolox was evangelized relatively slowly and the missionary campaign was largely in the hands of secular clergy. The work of conversion was initiated in 1527, the same year in which the Sierra Juárez was brought under Spanish military control. Although secular clergy had preceded him by more than two decades, the dominant figure in the initial period of conversion of the Chinantec was Fray de Saravia, who spent thirty years among the lowland Chinantec (Arroyo 1958[I]:127–38).

Fray Nicolás de la Barreda was the first cleric of prominence to work among the Chinantec of San Pedro Yolox, although he had been preceded by secular priests. His "Doctrina Christiana en lengua Chinanteca . . . ," a copy of which is still to be found in the ecclesiastical archives of the village, was the first written attempt to describe the principal mysteries of the Roman Catholic faith in the Chinantec language of San Pedro Yolox. Fray de la Barreda lived among the Yolox Chinantec from 1708 to 1728. In his "Respuesta Consultoria" he is said to have set down some impressions of the Chinantec of Yolox which can be considered among the earlier reflections of ethnographic interest (Cline 1959).

The Chinantla, more specifically the southeastern or lower Chinantla Grande, is the most varied and luxuriant botanical province of northeastern Oaxaca. It is the northern extremity of the Central American rain forest flora (Schultes 1941:101). Pioneer botanical research predates formal historical and anthropological inquiry.

Much of the literature pertaining to the Chinantla is devoted to the study of the difficult, tonal tongue of its inhabitants. Scholars have assigned it to various wider Oaxacan and Mexican classifications. Nicolás León (1903:282) and Francisco Belmar (1905:7, 8, 359, 360) assigned it to Zapotec, and Pimental (1903[II]:102–3) to Zapotec-Mixtec. Brinton (1891:144, 145, 340), although hypothesizing that it might be a surviving form of Olmec, later accorded it an independent status as did Mechling (1912:672) and Thomas and Swanton (1911:55). J. Alden Mason (1962:54, 77) calls attention to the work of C. H. Berendt, R. J. Weitlaner, and Jacques Soustelle who took vocabularies and copied the Barreda "Doctrina," presumably from the western highland Chinantec of San Pedro Yolox. A tentative grouping of Chinantec dialects has been proposed

(Weitlaner and Castro 1954:29, 30). Vocabularies from eight Chinantec pueblos appeared in Antonio Peñafiel's *Compendium of Vocabularies of Indigenous Languages of Mexico* in 1886 (Mechling 1912). However, vocabularies from the region of San Pedro Yolox are not represented in the Peñafiel collection.

The brief two-day visit of the third Starr field expedition in 1900 to San Juan Zautla and San Pedro Sochiapan, two Chinantec-speaking pueblos, initiated modern field research in the Chinantla. More specifically, the Starr field party took the first physical anthropological data on any Chinantec group (Starr 1902).

The first recorded archeological excavation in the Chinantla was made by Paul Henning on a field expedition directed by Mariano Espinosa in 1912 (Henning 1912:229–45). A contemporary and companion of Espinosa, Lorenzo del Peón Caso, however, has mounted the most extensive archeological inquiry in the region. His contributions to *Atlas archeológico de la República Mexicana* (1939) and his *Carta general y archeológica de Tuxtepec, Oaxaca* (1950) present the most extensive detailing of Chinantla sites.

The Mexican revolution occasioned an interruption in scholarly investigations in the Chinantla and the destruction of some data previously amassed. The late twenties, however, witnessed a resurgence of rather unspecialized interest in the region. Frances Toor's (1928) account of a brief stay in San Pedro Yolox provides some data on the folklore of the western highland Chinantec of the region of Yolox. J. Steward Lincoln (1939) conducted a more intensive investigation of the folklore and customs of the Chinantec-speaking group of eight pueblos in the lower Chinantla.

Much of the more specialized interest in the Chinantec derives from the field research conducted or organized by Robert J. Weitlaner. From 1934 to 1936 five such expeditions gathered data in the Chinantla, concentrating almost exclusively in areas outside the Yolox region. The fifth and final field expedition of this initial series of surveys touched briefly at San Pedro Yolox. The field phase of this research was only a month in length. San Pedro Yolox was but one of many pueblos on the extensive itinerary of this brief survey. Bernard Bevan, however, had been a member of all but one of the previous Weitlaner expeditions and he drew upon data thus collected for the basis of the first account of the Chinantec of any length (Bevan 1938).

The Bevan work deals in only the most peripheral fashion with the Yolox group and concentrates upon a relatively restricted subarea of the Chinantla, containing only a third of the region's population. His work deals almost exclusively with the Chinantec-speaking groups in the Valle Nacional in the District of Tuxtepec known collectively as the Wah-mi.* For more than a decade and a half the Bevan volume was the only book concerned exclusively with the Chinantec, a distinction which it maintained until the appearance of a monograph in 1954 on the Chinantec pueblos of Mayultianguis and Tlacoatzintepec (Weitlaner and Castro 1954).

A Wyclif Bible translator's brief description of the Chinantec of San Pedro Yolox based on his impressions gathered during his lengthy, intermittent residence in the village preceded the publication of the Weitlaner and Castro composite monograph by six years (Ford 1948).

Concurrent with the inception of the Papaloapan hydroelectric and general development scheme, the Republican agency charged with this project has commissioned ethnographic and economic research in the Papaloapan Basin which pertains to some Chinantec communities situated on tributaries of that important north Oaxacan waterway (Villa Rojas 1948:301–11).

Current ethnographic literature on the Chinantla reveals a startling congruity between the current ethnographic delineation and the traditional historical subdivision of the Chinantla. The Hu-me inhabit the region traditionally thought to have been the center of the classic Chinantec. The Wah-mi live in the southeast extremity of the lower Chinantla which is described

---

* Volume II of *The Chinantec*, which was to set forth Bevan's Yolox material together with data pertaining to other northern and western Chinantec-speaking groups, is as yet unpublished.

as the historical precinct of the emigrant Chinantec who separated from the classic Chinantec group in precontact antiquity. The Dza-mi, or Yolox group, are still found within their area of historic provenience in what was the ancient Chinantla Pichinche. The Usila Chinantec, to whom no collective name has yet been assigned, occupy approximately the same subregion of the Upper Chinantla once pertaining to the old "kingdom" of Usila.

The summary and desultory nature of the ethnographic literature on the region as a whole is paralleled by an equally spotty distribution of scholarly attention to the several ethnolinguistic subdivisions which constitute it. Modern research has tended to focus on Lower Chinantla groups. Though the first monographs dealt with communities in the Usila region, all but one of the five initial Weitlaner field parties worked exclusively in Hu-me and Wah-mi areas. The Bevan expedition, except for cursory views of the Dza-mi, or Yolox Chinantec, is almost exclusively concerned with the Hu-me and Wah-mi. These impressions of Bevan, the extremely brief and superficial accounts of a missionary and a folklorist and an even briefer, unpublished * report on the Cline field work in the autumn and winter of 1941–42 represent the totality of ethnographic literature on the site of this study.

* Subsequent to this writing, Cline's western Chinantec material has been published in the *Handbook of Middle American Indians*, edited by E. Z. Vogt, 1969, Vol. 7, pp. 545–52. Austin, University of Texas Press.

REFERENCES CITED

ALVAREZ AMÉZQUITA, JOSÉ. 1962. La oncocercosis como problema de salud pública. Salud Pública de México 4:909–13.

AMERICAN GEOGRAPHICAL SOCIETY OF NEW YORK. 1959. Sheet NE #14. Baltimore, A. Hoen and Company.

ARANDA VILLAMAYOR, CARLOS. 1963. Estudio epidemiológico de la oncocercosis en una área piloto en el estado de Oaxaca. Boletín Epidemiológico 27:51–69.

ARROYO, FRAY ESTEBAN. 1958. Los Dominicos, forjadores de la civilización. Vol. 1. Mexico, Camarena.

BANCROFT, HUBERT HOWE. 1874. Native Races of the Pacific States. Vol. 5. New York, D. Appleton and Company.

BELMAR, FRANCISCO. 1905. Lenguas indígenas de Mexico. Familia Mixteco-Zapoteca y sus relaciones con el Otomí. Familia Zoque-Mixe. Chontal. Huave y Mexicano. Mexico.

BEVAN, BERNARD. 1938. The Chinantec. Mexico, Pan American Institute of Geography and History.

BRINTON, DANIEL G. 1891. The American Race: A Linguistic Classification and Ethnographic Description of the Native Tribes of North and South America. New York.

CALDERÓN, V. M. 1917. Enfermedad nueva en Guatemala; resumen de la conferencia dada por el Dr. Rodolfo Robles. La Juventud Médica 17:97–116.

CHÁVEZ NÚÑEZ, MIGUEL. 1963. La epidemiologia de la oncocercosis en México. Boletín Epidemiológico 4:17–28.

CLINE, HOWARD F. 1952–53. Una subdivisión tentativa de los

Chinantecos históricos. Revista Mexicana de Estudios Antropológicos 13:281–86.

———. 1955. Civil Congregation of the Western Chinantla, New Spain, 1599–1603. The Americas 12:115–37.

———. 1956. The Chinantla of northeastern Oaxaca, Mexico. Bio-bibliographical notes on modern investigation. In Estudios Antropológicos publicados en homenaje al doctor Manuel Gamio. Edited by Eusebio Dávalos Hurtado and Ignacio Bernal. Mexico, Universidad Autónoma de Mexico-Sociedad Mexicana de Antropología: 635–56.

———. 1957. Problems of Mexican ethno-history: the ancient Chinantla. Hispanic American Historical Review 37:273–95.

———. 1959. Nicolás de la Barreda and his works on the Chinantec Indians of Mexico. Separate from the Papers of the Bibliographical Society of America. Vol. 53, First Quarter.

———. 1961. Mapas y lienzos of the Colonial Chinantec Indians, Oaxaca, Mexico. Reprinted from To William Cameron Townsend, in the XXV Anniversary of the Summer Institute of Linguistics: 49–77. Mitla, Mexico.

CRUZ, WILFRIDO C. 1946. Oaxaca recóndita. Mexico, Beatriz de Silva.

DE LA FUENTE, JULIO. 1949. Yalalag una villa Zapoteca serrana. Mexico, Museo Nacional de Antropología.

DÍAZ DEL CASTILLO, BERNAL. 1965. The Discovery and Conquest of Mexico. Genaro García, editor. Translated by A. P. Maudsley. New York, Noonday Press.

ESPINOSA, MARIANO. 1961. Apuntes históricos de las tribus Chinantecas, Matzatecas y Popolucas (1910). Reprinted in Papeles de la Chinantla. Vol. 3. Mexico, Museo Nacional de Antropología.

ESQUIVEL, DIEGO DE. 1579. Relación de la Chinantla. In Papeles de la Nueva España. Edited by Francisco Paso y Troncoso. Madrid, 1905 4:58–68.

FORD, STANLEY L. 1948. The Chinantec tribe. Boletín Indigenista 8:290–98.

FOSTER, GEORGE M. 1942. A Primitive Mexican Economy. Monographs of the American Ethnological Society, New York, J. J. Augustin.

———. 1962. Traditional Cultures and the Impact of Technological Change. New York, Harper and Row.

GARCÍA SÁNCHEZ, FELIPE AND MIGUEL CHÁVEZ NÚÑEZ. 1962. Epidemiologia de la oncocercosis en México. Salud Pública de México 5:939–58.

GAY, JOSÉ ANTONIO. 1933. Historia de Oaxaca (1881). 2d edition. Vol. 1. Oaxaca, Talleres tipográficos del gobierno.

GRACIDA, MANUEL. 1883. Cuadros sinópticos de los pueblos, haciendas y ranchos del Estado Libre y Soberano de Oaxaca. Oaxaca.

HENNING, PAUL. 1912. Informe del colector de documentos etnológicos sobre el excursión a Tuxtepec, Oaxaca. Mexico, Museo Nacional, Buletín I, no. 11.

HUXLEY, ALDOUS. 1960. Beyond the Mexique Bay (1934). 2d edition. New York, Vintage Books.

ITURRIBARRIA, JOSÉ F. 1955. Oaxaca en la historia. Mexico, Editorial Stylo. Publications of the University of Benito Juárez, Oaxaca.

LEÓN, NICOLÁS. 1903. Familias lingüísticas de Mexico. Mexico, Museo Nacional, Anales VII.

LEVI YITZCHAK ISAAC BEN MEIR. 1816. Kedushat Levi. Berdycher.

LEWIS, OSCAR. 1960. Tepoztlán Village in Mexico. New York, Holt, Rinehart and Winston, Inc.

——. 1963. Life in a Mexican Village: Tepoztlán Restudied. Urbana, University of Illinois Press.

LINCOLN, J. STEWARD. 1939. The southeastern Chinantla of Mexico. Scientific Monthly 49:57–65.

MASON, J. ALDEN. 1962. The native languages of Middle America. In The Maya and Their Neighbors. Charles L. Hay, editor. New York, D. Appleton-Century Company.

MAZZOTTI, LUIS. 1962. Tratamiento de la oncocercosis. Salud Pública de México 4:1047–54.

MECHLING, WILLIAM H. 1912. The Indian linguistic stocks of Oaxaca, Mexico. American Anthropologist 14:643–82.

MEXICO. SECRETARÍA DE INDUSTRIA Y COMERCIO. DIRECCIÓN GENERAL DE ESTADÍSTICA. 1963. VIII censo general de población, 1960. Vol. 1. Oaxaca.

MONTEMAYOR, FELIPE. 1954. Los efectos de la onchocercosis en la población de Acacoyahua, Chis. Mexico, Secretaría de Educación Pública.

OCHOTERENA, ISAAC. 1948. Biologic medium and social conditions in onchocercosis zones. Boletín Indigenista 8:277–85.

ORTIZ MARIOTTE, CARLOS. 1963. Historia de la lucha antioncocercosa en México. Boletín Epidemiológico 27:7–15.

PEÓN CASO, LORENZO DEL. 1939. Atlas arqueológico de la República Mexicana. Mexico, Pan American Institute of Geography and History, publication 41:151–84.

——. 1950. Carta general y arqueológica del Distrito de Tuxtepec, Oaxaca. Mexico.

PÉREZ GARCÍA, ROSENDO. 1956. La Sierra Juárez. Vol. 1. Mexico, Gráfica Cervantina.

PIMENTEL, FRANCISCO. 1903. Obras completas. Vol. 2. Mexico.

QUIJADA, HERNANDO. 1579. Relación de Ucila. In Papeles de la Nueva España. Edited by Francisco Paso y Troncoso. Madrid, 1905, 4:58–68.

QUIROZ, ALONZO DE. 1603. Congregación de el pueblo y cabezera de San Pedro Yolos Xiniquila, y de sus estancias. . . . Cited in Civil congregation of the western Chinantla, New Spain, 1599–1603. Cline 1955:128.

REDFIELD, ROBERT. 1960. The Little Community and Peasant Society and Culture. Chicago, University of Chicago Press.

RIBERA, JUAN DE. 1599. De la demarcación y visita que se hizo de las cabezeras de Yollosinequila y San Pablo Macuiltianguis. Mexico, Archivo general de la nación. Tierras, 64, no. 4.

RUBEL, ARTHUR J. 1955. Ritual relationships in Ojitlán, Mexico. American Anthropologist 57:1038–40.

SALAZAR MALLÉN, MARIO. 1963. Los síntomas cutáneos de la oncocercosis. Salud Pública de México 4:1071–74.

SAN PEDRO YOLOX. ARCHIVO GENERAL. 1884. Historia del pueblo de Yolox en su congregación en el año de 1603.

——. 1958–63. Birth Registry.

——. 1963. Head of Household Census.

——. 1963. Inhabitant Census.

SCHULTES, RICHARD E. 1941. The meaning and usage of the Mexican place-name "Chinantla." Cambridge, Harvard University Botanical Museum Leaflets, 9:101–16.

STARR, FREDERICK. 1900. Notes upon the ethnography of southern Mexico. Davenport, Iowa. Academy of Natural Sciences, Proceedings. Vol. 8.

———. 1902. The physical characters of the Indians of southern Mexico. Chicago, Separate from the University of Chicago Decennial Publications. Vol. 4.

STRONG, R. P., J. H. SANDGROUND, J. C. BEQUAERT, AND OCHOA M. MUÑOZ. 1934. Onchocerciasis with Special Reference to the Central American Form of the Disease. Cambridge, Harvard University Press.

THOMAS, CYRUS, AND JOHN R. SWANTON. 1911. Indian languages of Mexico and Central America and their geographical distribution, accompanied with a linguistic map. Washington, Smithsonian Institution, Bureau of American Ethnology, Bulletin 44.

TOOR, FRANCES. 1928. Gentes y escuelas de la Sierra de Juárez. Mexican Folkways 4:119–29.

TORROELLA, JAVIER. 1962. Las alteraciones oculares de la oncocercosis. Salud Pública de México 4:1039–45.

VARGAS, LUIS. 1962. Transmisión de onchocerca volvulus en México. Salud Pública de México 4:959–69.

VILLA ROJAS, ALFONSO. 1948. El papel de la antropología en las obras del Papaloapan, Mexico. América Indígena 8:301–11.

WEITLANER, IRMGARD. 1952–53. El quechquemitl y el huipil. Revista Mexicana de Estudios Antropológicos 13:241–57.

WEITLANER, ROBERT J. 1939. Los Chinantecos. Revista Mexicana de Estudios Antropológicos 3:195–216.

———. 1940. Notes on Chinantec ethnography. El México Antiguo 5:161–75.

———. 1951. Notes on the social organization of Ojitlán, Oaxaca. In Ensayos en homenaje a don Alfonso Caso. Mexico: 441–55.

———. 1964. Supervivencias de la religión y magia pre-hispánicas en Guerrero y Oaxaca. Mexico, 35th International Congress of Americanists (1962), Actas y Memorias 2:557–63.

WEITLANER, ROBERT J., AND CARLOS A. CASTRO. 1954. Mayultianguis and Tlacoatzintepec. In Papeles de la Chinantla, Vol. 1. Mexico, Instituto Nacional de Antropología e Historia.

WOLF, ERIC R. 1962. Sons of the Shaking Earth. Chicago, University of Chicago Press.

WORLD HEALTH ORGANIZATION. 1962. Bulletin. Onchocerciasis and filariasis. Volume 27, no. 4–5. Geneva.